6983-3

D0664164

Hands

Other books by Enid Hoffman

Develop Your Psychic Skills
Huna: A Beginner's Guide

HANDS

A Complete Guide to Palmistry
by Enid Hoffman

A Division of Schiffer Publishing
4880 Lower Valley Rd.
Atglen, PA 19310 USA

Published by Whitford Press
A Division of Schiffer Publishing, Ltd.
4880 Lower Valley Road
Atglen, PA 19310 USA
Phone: (610) 593-1777 Fax: (610) 593-2002
E-mail: schifferbk@aol.com
Please visit our website catalog at
www.schifferbooks.com
or write for a free catalog.
This book may be purchased from the publisher.
Please include $3.95 postage.
Try your bookstore first.

In Europe, Schiffer books are distributed by
Bushwood Books
6 Marksbury Avenue
Kew Gardens
Surrey TW9 4JF England
Phone: 44 (0)208-392-8585; Fax: 44 (0)208-392-9876
E-mail: Bushwd@aol.com

We are interested in hearing from authors
with book ideas on related subjects.

Hands: A Complete Guide to Palmistry
by Enid Hoffman

Copyright © 1983 Enid Hoffman
Cover design copyright © 1983 Para Research, Inc.

All rights reserved. No part of this book may be
reproduced or used in any form or by any means—graphic,
electronic, or mechanical, including photocopying,
mimeographing, recording, taping, or information storage
and retrieval systems—without written permission from
the publisher. A reviewer may quote brief passages.

Library of Congress Catalog Card Number: 83-62043
International Standard Book Number: 0-914918-48-6

Typeset in 10 pt. Paladium on Compugraphic 7500

Edited by Anne Driscoll and Marah Ren
Cover design by Ralph Poness and Todd Sweet
Illustrations by Robert Killam
Graphics by Robert Killam and Marlene Comet
Typeset by Sinikka Nogelo
256 pages

Published by Whitford Press, a division of
Schiffer Publishing, Ltd.

Manufactured in the United States of America.

Contents

List of Figures

Introduction

Since the time when our primitive ancestors first grasped, clawed, or dug with rudimentary fingers, many myths have developed about the distinctive meanings assigned to the right and left hands. Several cultures, like the ancient Chinese, viewed the functioning of the hands as contrasting but balanced in importance. However, most other cultures did not. They believed the right hand to be superior, the left inferior.

Various groups have defined the left hand as disreputable, radical, murderous, bewitched, profane, impure, feeble. To Moslems, touching another with the left hand is an insult. The Maori people of New Zealand equate the left side of the body with death, and protect themselves by wearing charms and amulets on their left arms.

Many modern religions have further promoted the myth of the superiority of the right hand by glorifying the "right hand of God." Many religious paintings depict the right hand pointing toward heaven, the left toward hell. In the famous Michelangelo painting, *The Creation*, on the ceiling of the Sistine Chapel, it is the right hand of God touching Adam, giving the gift of life.

Rather than a belief that both hands are equal, we find a nearly global view that the right hand is superior. The prejudice that haunts the left hand can be found rooted in language, as well. The Anglo-Saxon root for *lyft* (left) literally means weak or broken. The French word for left, *gauche*, means socially inept or awkward, as in a "left-handed compliment." The almost forgotten definition of the word *sinister* as left, or to the left, comes from the Old French and Latin usage in divination, when the left side was considered inauspicious. The word continues to have evil connotations such as wrong, underhanded, dishonest, corrupt, disastrous or injurious.

Conversely, right (or *riht* in Old English) means morally upright, correct, normal, or genuine. These definitions of right and left, which help us to begin to understand the myths about the right and left hands, differ radically from the view of the Chinese, who believe the *complementary* forces of Yin and Yang can represent a balance, even in the hands.

We find examples in our own society where left-handedness is a condition to be cured and schoolteachers and parents try to convert their left-handers to the RIGHT way of writing and using their hands.

It is unfortunate that palmistry, the study of the lines of the hands, has historically subscribed to the belief that the right hand is "masculine" and positive, while the left hand is considered "feminine" and negative. The phrase, "the left hand of fortune" means something that brings bad luck and is an example of this line of reasoning.

However, recent research into the functions of the two hemispheres of the brain provides some clue as to the reason the right hand has been viewed as superior. Since the revolutionary "split-brain" studies conducted during the 1950s and 60s at the California Institute of Technology by Roger W. Sperry and his associates, scientists have come to believe that the left side of the brain controls the right side of the body and vice versa, but that both hemispheres of the human brain are involved in higher cognitive functions and the two hemispheres simply employ different methods or modes of processing information.

The left brain/right side controls the intellectual, rational and objective reasoning functions. Conversely, scientists believe that creativity, intuition and emotions reside in the right hemisphere, which controls the left side.

The majority of cultures throughout history have encouraged rational, intellectual thought, rather than emotional development. So lies the clue—it is the rational thinking person, the one who has developed his or her left brain/right side who is a cultural hero/ine, not the person ruled by his or her emotions. Emphasis on development of left-brain attributes has been encouraged by many societies. These left-brain skills are usually considered "masculine."

However, centuries before scientists had revealed the capacities of the two hemispheres, the ancient Chinese had already begun to understand the Yin and the Yang duality of the whole. Yin/Yang refers to the complementary relationship between the traditionally rational "male" qualities (yang/right hand) and the traditionally emotional "female" qualities (yin/left hand). Although Eastern society was male-dominated, "feminine" pursuits such as music, art and poetry were encouraged. The result was a cultural balance between the powers of intellect and intuition.

I propose a reconsideration of the meanings of the two hands toward a new paradigm of hand analysis—*holistic* and *balanced*. Moving away from old concepts of the right and left hands, this book adopts a holistic view of the hands, in regard to their complementary relationship, their relationship to the whole body.

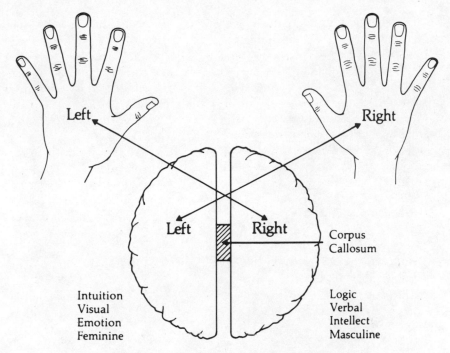

Left

Right

Left Right

Corpus
Callosum

Intuition
Visual
Emotion
Feminine

Logic
Verbal
Intellect
Masculine

Figure I-1. The Hemispheres of the Brain

This book intends to provide a "balanced" outline of *hand analysis* in which the complementary functions of both hands will be reconsidered. This new perspective is based in part on the findings that the two distinct hemispheres of the brain govern opposite sides of the body.

This text will also be "holistic" in that it will provide the meanings behind nearly all aspects of the hand and its structure. Although this book includes information on "palmistry," it is not strictly a book about palms. Instead, we use hand analysis to discuss the "whole" meaning of the hands, interpreting finger and hand size, color, shape, dominance and dexterity, as well as fingernail size, shape and shading. This book will also examine the meanings of various fingerprint formations (known as dermaglyphs) and the more commonly considered lines of the palms.

The holistic method of hand analysis explained in this book will not only consider your emotional state, but also your physical health, since the two are virtually inseparable.

By coupling a revision of old ideas with an expansion of new ideas, this method of hand analysis becomes a promising blend of the wisdom of the ancients and the knowledge of the New Age.

1

The Hands

The lines, wrinkles, and shape of your hands are the road maps to your individual potential; however, in order to read the map you first need to understand the territory. The back of the hand, the terrain of the hand itself, or hand proper, is the area from the wrist to the fingers. Beneath the surface of the skin lie the five bones of the metacarpus. Each of the four fingers flex at the joints of the three phalanges, beginning with the first, or uppermost phalange.

The joints between the phalanges are called knots, and are either smooth or knotted (gnarled). The thumb also has three phalanges, although the third, called the Mount of Venus, is one of five metacarpal bones forming the palm proper.

The palm side is called the Map of the Hand. It includes the surface from the wrist to the base of the fingers, and contains the mounts, rivers (lines), islands and plains.

When facing the palm side of your hand, imagine a line running from the tip of your middle finger down through the palm and ending in the middle of the wrist, dividing the hand in half. The thumb side of one half is called the *radial* side, and the other is called the *ulna* side. They derive these labels from a set of nerves that flow down through the arm culminating in the hand.

Looking at your palm, you will notice that the flesh rises and falls, creating valleys and mountains in miniature. Each one of these has a name. In addition to valleys and mountains, there are plains or level places. Each hand varies, but each hand also has general similarities.

Elevations, called mounts, rise at the base of each finger. The rest of the palm is subdivided into the Quadrangle and Triangle along certain lines of the hands, both of which form the Hollow of the Hand.

The shapes of the tips of both the fingers and the thumbs are helpful indicators in understanding the meaning of our hands. Their shapes are classified in four forms: pointed, conical, square and spatulate.

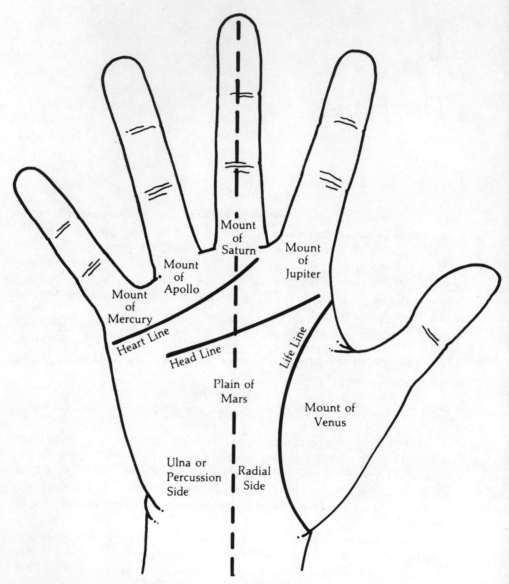

Figure 1-1. Map of the Hand

The message that the map of our hands provides in a physical form first originates in the brain. The brain sends its messages along three nerve transit systems. These major systems travel along the arms into the hands.

The ulna nerves travel from the elbow to the little finger, ring finger and half the middle finger. The radial nerves fill the other digits, including the thumb, forefinger and half the middle finger. The radial and ulna nerves are found on the backside of the hands, while the third major system, the median nerves, involve the palm and underside of the fingers.

The median system controls the motion of the thumb, middle and third finger, and is the source of sensation through touch. The median system contains more peccunian bodies (cells that transmit touch) than any other nerves. Our sense of touch is keenest in the thumb, index, middle and ring fingers, with the little finger being the least sensitive.

Brain to Hand

What then are the mesages sent from the brain to the hands?

The brain consists of two halves or hemispheres connected by nerve fibers. Each hemisphere, generally the size of a clenched fist, controls the opposite side of the body.

Therefore, the left hand is connected to the right hemisphere of the neo-cortex part of the brain and the right hand is connected to the left hemisphere.

Apparently, separate and different messages are sent from each side of the brain. Brain surgeries performed for the treatment of various seizures show that when the two hemispheres are severed, the halves continue to function separately.

Therefore, a patient might be able to read the word "bread" using the right eye (left brain), but could not recognize or imagine it! Likewise, when such a patient is seeing with the left eye (right brain), he or she could draw a loaf of bread but would be unable to say the word!

"Split-brain surgery" has also revealed that each hemisphere is the center of different but complementary functions; the right hemisphere is the seat of imagination, creativity and intuition, while the left half is the center of logical, intellectual thought.

Therefore, the creative, emotional concerns of an individual, having been given birth in the brain's right hemisphere and transmitted along the nerves, can be translated in the left hand. Likewise, the right hand will represent the intellectual messages of the left half of the brain.

Both messages need recognition; one is not complete without the other. To illustrate this, think about the way you hear people speak. Your left hemisphere listens, hears the words and understands the meaning of what is spoken. It can easily remember what was said and what was meant by the words.

Your right hemisphere listens to the sounds of the voice, registering the tone, the timbre, the quality and the silences. It translates these into information about the inner experience of the speaker and the shared feelings.

Together, the distinctive capacity of each hemisphere works to decipher a "whole" message. Consciously, we classify people by their appearance and our objective experience of them, while beneath the conscious level, we respond to their inner feelings, their interior. Think of how many messages would be lost if we only listened to the words people spoke instead of the emotion behind the words. The right hemisphere (left hand) then relates the essence within things and the emotional content and pattern we perceive in people and objects.

For example, can you recall the sound of another person's voice? Do you ever consciously listen to that sound or sounds? Try to recall a recent interaction and see if you can remember the *sound* of the conversation. That memory is an example of your right hemisphere at work.

It is understandable that painters, who have greater right brain development (creativity), do not perceive the world in an orderly fashion, but as an arena of colors, light, shadows and feelings. Likewise, a mathematician is more likely to be aware of the regular tempo of Rock-a-Bye-Baby than the notes and music of the lullaby.

The information we receive through all five of our senses is processed in this dual fashion by the two halves of the brain. For example, our left hemisphere (right hand) identifies the smell, while the right hemisphere (left hand) experiences its essence and nature. So, when the left brain identifies the fresh clean scent of newly cut grass, the right brain is attaching an emotional association to it—perhaps the high spirits and hopes of spring.

The life that we experience through the complementary capacities of the two brain hemispheres is represented in our opposite hands. Understanding the relationship and differences between the two hands is vitally important in your effort to understand what each of the hands represents. And through that understanding of the two hands, you can better understand the various sides of your self; which side is underdeveloped, which is overdeveloped and which emotions you may have ignored completely. It is truly a process of discovery.

Your Yin/Yang Hand

A study of the Chinese *I Ching*, or Book of Changes, helps us to understand the duality of the hands. This ancient and profound book of wisdom helps us to understand that with a line, duality comes into the world, for the line creates an above and below, a right and a left, a front and a back. It creates the world of opposites, of which we are all a part. At any time, the influence of one side of this duality may be stronger or more predominant than the other. A balance of both is most desirable.

Yin/Yang represents the duality of the whole. The dark/light, feminine/masculine, yielding/firm aspects of each creation. What is frequently depicted as the traditional yin/yang symbol—☯—is actually one of the earliest attempts to represent the *tao*, the "great primal beginning" of the Oriental philosophy of the one in the many.

In the text of the *I Ching* itself, the yang principle is represented as "the firm" and the yin principle as "the yielding." All other attributions now associated with the yin/yang symbol were added to the Commentaries on the text after the Book of Changes had been used as a divinatory oracle for some time.

The yin principle of the *I Ching* is associated in hand analysis with the left hand and when predominant can be seen in the oval-shaped hands of intuitive, reflective individuals. The yang principle is associated with the right hand and when predominant is reflected in individuals with square-shaped hands and active egos.

The symbol for the left hand is the circle, the symbol for the right hand is the square. The circle clearly represents the primary, feeling force within the left hand—infinite, without beginning or end. Hands, fingers and nails that reflect this shape with an oval appearance often indicate individuals with overtly emotional tendencies. These individuals often make contributions in the fields of art, music, drama, communication and social services.

The square, symbol of the secondary force, the right hand, represents the earth and all its objective manifestations. Hands, fingers or nails that reflect this shape with a square appearance often indicate individuals who work with their hands to produce material goods and services such as farmers, construction workers, miners, machine operators.

The primary and secondary forces are complementary components of the process of creation. The elementary power of intuition and visualization creates a need for the physical manifestation to complete the work. The left hand begets and the right hand brings to birth in the objective world. The left-brain/right-hand function is that of analytical, rational processing, while the right-brain/left-hand function is a more spatial, global and intuitive form of processing. The left hand/inner self "feels" and the right hand/ego manifests those feelings in a concrete way. When and if either tries to subjugate the other, the conflict begins. The *whole* self—feminine/masculine, dark/light, yielding/firm, intuitive/rational—is the continuous transformation of each force into the other, a flow of continuous changes forming one harmonious whole.

What Our Hands Reveal

As the fingerprints of every individual's hands are unique, so are the hands themselves. Each hand reveals and reflects a unique set of personal traits, characteristics and tendencies represented in size, shape and structure.

Every hand has a skeletal structure which may have grown straight, as it naturally will, or may have been stunted or warped in its growth. Over the skeletal structure lays a fleshy covering and an outer surface of skin. The hands have five fingers and fingernails, which grow to various lengths, shapes and textures. All of these factors indicate personal features about the individual.

Unseen, the nervous systems that lie below the surface create outward effects. We perceive these as the lines that run across the palmar and inner finger patterns, commonly known as prints. These visible patterns and programs tell us of the flow of mental, emotional and physical energies by which we react and respond to our environment.

Our hands reflect the processes that occur in the opposite hemispheres of our brains. The left hand is patterned by the electrical impulses that constantly flow through the right hemisphere of the neo-cortex, while the right hand reflects the process that occurs in the left hemisphere of the neo-cortex.

Like the hieroglyphics of the ancient Egyptians, it is possible to decipher the meanings of these patterns. The hands can be a mirror of our thought processes. What our hands reveal is a record of past actions, thought and feelings. Once we learn the meanings of the individual symbols found in our hands, we can then know the message our hands provide.

The skin carvings on the face of our hands are called *dermaglyphs*. We are born with unchangeable dermaglyphs. Some researchers now believe the dermaglyphic patterns will provide clues to the individual's particular traits; their genetic tendencies and inherited characteristics.

Unlike the permanent records of the dermaglyphs, our hands also reveal more momentary messages as well. The muscles in our hands are a means of communicating momentary emotional and mental states. These inner states of being can be translated by reading the motions of the muscles. Tense muscles indicate inner tensions, relaxed muscles indicate inner relaxation.

By considering all the above, as well as many other aspects of your hands, you may uncover the secrets of your self. By observing if your fingers are short or long, you may learn whether you are sensitive or not. By feeling your hands for smooth skin, you may discover whether you are aesthetically inclined or unaware. By seeing if your fingernails are broad or small, you may know how broad-minded you really are. These are but several examples from an abundance of information revealed through the symbols of your hands.

The dermaglyphs are not the cause of your emotions and ways of thinking; rather, they are a reflection of them. Understanding these patterns helps you to understand yourself.

Consciousness of the Hands

The components of the "sound" of a conversation illustrate the two ways messages are interpreted. The message of the spoken word and the message implied by the timbre and inflection of the voice are both parts of the communication process. The right hand, through the left brain, interprets the objective message, while the left hand, through the right brain, gives clues to the "silent message."

As such, the left hand is considered the non-verbal, "silent" hand. Its mode of communciation tends to be a telepathic connection rather than one based on objective data or words.

Dreaming is a function represented by the left hand. Although dreams sometimes contain words, more often images carry the profound meaning of the dream.

In contrast, the right hand represents the center of the ego, the ego that loves the sound of its own voice. It hears sounds while ignoring the silences for it is fearful of silence. An ego-centered person avoids "the still, silent voice within," that expression of the left hand; and instead, seeks to drown it in chattering noise.

If the right hand views silence as the absence of sound, rather than an opportunity to hear the voice within, it is most likely overlooking the messages connected to the left hand.

The left hand represents the dreamer and the right hand the doer. The right hand is related to daytime, waking consciousness. It reflects concern with the visible, audible world and how to function in it.

Conversely, the left hand reflects the invisible, inaudible and subtle world we experience subconsciously. This is the world of daydreams, and waking trances in which our concentration drifts from ego-centered experience. Dream states, meditations and hypnotic trances are also examples of states in which awareness is an arena of emotion and feelings, based on images rather than words.

In a research project reported in *Biological Psychiatry* (Vol. 13, No. 6), twenty right-handed men and women were asked to listen to a series of sounds. Wearing headphones, the subjects heard different one-syllable sounds in both ears simultaneously, and then related what they heard. In normal waking consciousness, they reported what they heard in their right ear much more frequently than what they heard in the left ear. The "right-ear advantage" is due to the ego-awareness of the left hemisphere during waking consciousness.

Strangely enough, when the subjects were hypnotized, they described sounds more often heard by the left ear. This may indicate the connection between an altered state of consciousness and the right hemisphere.

An examination of consciousness provides other clues to the messages of the hands. In everyday waking consciousness, the mind is most aware of experience as a sequential event. Time, as experienced by the left hemisphere, is a sequence of past, present and future.

But for those of you who have ever experienced an altered state of consciousness, such as hypnosis, meditation or daydreaming, you are aware that the past, present and future fades away into *now*.

For the most part, society dictates that awareness is present only during waking consciousness. However, anyone who has undergone hypnosis will tell you that the subconscious is *always* aware, and even while we sleep, we generally tend to overdevelop skills associated with the left brain and ignore experience available to us through the right brain.

However, our left hand can help us develop that part of ourselves. The maps of our left hand can provide valuable information about the workings of our right hemisphere. Using this, we can experience a fully balanced and satisfying existence.

Primary and Secondary Hands

Although it is clear that we experience the objective world in sharp contrast to the subjective world, using both hemispheres of our brain, which of these two realms is first?

The inner self, represented by the left hand, is the realm of experience where emotions are dominant. Emotions are ceaseless, for as quickly as we feel one, another bursts forth. The inner self is also the seat of creativity. The inner "natural" self of emotions is continually seeking avenues of expression. However, since it is an "inner" realm, it lacks the ability to express itself directly. Creative expression requires the aid of the outer self, the ego represented by the right hand.

As such, it is the left hand (the inner self) which we consider primary. The right hand, as the servant of the left, is considered secondary. The terms *primary* and *secondary* do not connote a level of importance. Both are necessary, both are of equal importance and both are required to create the whole.

The left hand represents the primary source, the space of ceaseless feeling, endless being. It reflects the inner space where time is now, ever being. But it cannot "create" or "express" unless the right hand cooperates.

The left hand mirrors the process of *being*, the right hand the process of *becoming*. The left hand holds the potential for transformation, the right hand is active in changing.

The outer self represented in the right hand can become the servant of the feeling self, expressing in outward objective form the feelings that arise every moment from the inner source. Or, it can ignore, restrict and suppress the feeling side.

The feelings from the primary source, represented in the left hand, flood the physical body as they are experienced. The secondary hand, the right hand, determines whether that emotional force will be expressed or contained. If held in suspension, the muscles reflect a state of tension and rigidity. If released into action, the physical body remains healthy and graceful. Our hands then reflect a state of relaxed health or tension.

The complementary force of both hands working together holds tremendous power. Together, the transformation possible in the left hand can become a reality with the help of the right hand. So why would the right hand, as an indicator of the left side of the brain, ever inhibit the expression of the left hand?

Our society is one in which clear, logical reasoning powers are applauded, while emotions are considered a hindrance to the real work of the mind. Our culture abounds with ego-centered individuals who continually suppress their feelings. "Control yourself!" society cries. "Keep your emotions hidden," it commands. Our culture has taught us to fear our own selves, to submerge our inner experience.

Too often the outcome of this conflict is dominance by the right hand and left brain in service to the egotistical outer self, expressed by the left hand and right brain. Meanwhile, the inner self is smothered, restrained and unable to express itself. Our culture approves of a strong ego that controls the natural urges of the inner self in service to the concerns of the ego. Our educational system encourages development of the individual who is groomed to serve society, rather than serve the inner self, with his or her intellectual abilities.

However, true self-realization occurs when the *whole* self is developed. The ego becomes aware that it exists to serve the self within, as well as society. Only after the individual has learned to express his or her own true self can he or she communicate that expression to others. Cultural advances are truly the result of the egotistical self bringing to fruition the wisdom gained through intuition and insight.

Hand analysis can aid you in your search for self-realization and appreciation of your left-hand potentials, but what happens if cooperation does not exist between the two hands?

Many experts who have studied stress claim there is a strong relationship between the denial and suppression of feeling exhibited by the so-called "Type A" personality and a wide variety of ailments, such as hypertension and heart failure.

The hands can provide clues about the relationship between health and the emotions. For instance, experts in hand analysis see a correlation between the liver (as represented in the ulna side of the palm) and the manifestation of emotional disappointments and conflicts with others. The hands can also show evidence of an enlarged spleen. This indicates an individual who has been controlled against his or her will, or someone who has challenged authority.

The health line is also called the liver line and actually reflects disturbances in health due to emotional relationships with the outer world. A lack of love from the environment can create a health line that is very distinct and easily seen.

Thus, it is obvious that your hands are a reflection of you and your health. Through the study of your hands you can come closer to an understanding of who you truly are.

2

Hand Dominance

It is a fact than 90 percent of the American population eats, writes and works with their right hands. It is then a staggering majority who make their way in the world using their right hands. However, hand dominance is not just a matter of which hand lifts the pen, raises the fork or holds the hammer—it is more complex. Right- or left-handedness is only one of several tests for hand dominance.

As was discussed in the first chapter, the two hemispheres of the brain are connected to the opposite sides of the body. The left hemisphere, which is the seat of analytical thinking and intellectual concerns, governs the right side of the body. Conversely, the right side of the brain, where intuition and creativity reside, influences the left side of the body.

Hand dominance is really an indication of how the two hemispheres share control over one body, one person. Although handedness provides a very strong indicator of dominance, it is only one of several considerations. We use each hand for a variety of skills, yet some of us are extremely right-handed (with little use of the left hand) and others are markedly left-handed (with few skills in our right hand).

The existence of an overwhelming majority of right-handers is probably due to our culture, in which our survival is directly dependent on how well we speak, read and analyze. The use and understanding of words is absolutely essential to success in the objective world. Therefore, the hand that represents the ego-centered objective self, the right, is usually the dominant one. However, if we were to test 90 percent of the population, we would find a wide range in the degree that people were fixed within right-hand dominance. A surprising number would in fact use their left hands for any number of tasks. Perhaps some would even have mixed hand dominance.

The hand that we most often use to grasp, hold and reach in the early stages of infancy, and perhaps even when we are born, is the hand which we will continue to naturally prefer. This hand preference is unchangeable. Even for those left-handers whose unrelenting parents tried to coax them into using their right hands, *left-hand dominance* will remain unaffected. This is why hand dominance cannot be decided solely by determining which hand is used most often.

There are other tests to determine the degree to which either hand is dominant. Testing for hand dominance is the method of determining to what extent the person is influenced by the right or left hemispheres. Although it is impossible for the left-handed person to be determined as right-hand dominant (or vice versa), you can find a wide range in the degree to which a person uses that left hand.

In light of the fact that our two brain hemispheres control opposite sides of the body, it should be no surprise that there are other known points of dominance in various parts of the body. For example, it has been found that there is eye, ear and foot dominance. Anthropologists have suggested that people with mixed dominance seem to be more stable than those whose dominance is completely right-sided or entirely left-sided.

Just for fun, try an experiment to determine your foot dominance. Stand with your back to the wall and your feet side by side. Impulsively step out and walk ahead. Which foot took the first step? That is your dominant foot!

If you are right-handed, it will increase your "type" if your right foot stepped out first. Likewise, a left-handed person who walks first with the left foot will have stronger tendencies associated with the right brain. If hand and foot are reversed in dominance, it represents an attempt by the body toward a balance, an attempt to make us two-sided people instead of one-sided.

Types of Hand Dominance

Right Hand. People with dominant right-handedness are strong in their development of the intellect, reasoning powers and practicality. They are likely to suppress feelings and control the expression of their inner, natural self. Right-handers nurture a strong ego and tend to develop in culturally approved ways. Generally, they stick to the dictates of convention and are concerned about what others think of them. In this way, they are often very successful by societal standards. Those with right-hand dominance use logical building blocks, which are necessary to consequential thinking. By assembling known facts to come to a conclusion, the belief system of the ego is firmed up. Right-handed people are the workers of the world, the backbone of society.

Left Hand. Left-handed people favor intuitive hunches and inspirations. They are acutely aware of how others feel. Because their own emotions are more important than what others expect of them, they often are rebellious. In general, I have found left-handers to be remarkably innovative and original in their thinking. This is probably related to the way the right hemisphere, which dominates the left hand, experiences life, primarily processing impressions of reality as mental images of sight, sound, touch, taste and smell.

Since left-handers are intuitive, answers come to them without doing the tedious work involved in the step-by-step procedures of problem solving. As a result, they have frequently been labelled slow by our educational system, which emphasizes that we know *how* to solve a problem with rational sequential thinking rather than knowing what the answer is. Left-handers are labelled "lucky guessers," an unacceptable way of life to right-handed society.

If you are left-handed, you are in a group that comprises a fraction, about 10 percent, of the population here in the United States. You are called a southpaw, and even sinister, although that label was more common in the nineteenth century when left was synonomous with evil and ominous occurences.

Not so long ago, left-handed writers were forced to write with their right hands. Now, although left-handedness is more accepted, left-handers may still have difficulty adapting to a world designed for right-handers. For example, using a pair of scissors or a can opener can be an almost impossible task for a left-handed person.

Left-handers are unique people. No left-hander is exactly like another in his or her own handedness. How each person uses their two hands to function in the world varies from one to another. Many left-handers are ambidextrous, or nearly so. In adapting to the design of the right-handed world, they may compensate by using their right hands more frequently. In fact, nearly every left-hander uses their right hand much more than a right-hander will use his or her left.

Two different sets of muscles govern the two areas involved with the hands: hand strength and hand dexterity. Unlike the right-hander who has developed dexterity and strength in the right hand, the left-handed person may develop one set of muscles in each hand. Therefore, the person who writes with the left hand may use the right hand to unscrew the lid from an impossible jar.

A higher percentage of lefties are stutterers, slow learners and faulty readers as children because of the left hand's connection to the right hemisphere, which prefers the language of images rather than the written and spoken word.

Left-handers tend to be more rebellious and non-conformist than right-handers, but this could be the result of the discrimination they suffer. It is not surprising that left-handers might reject a world which constantly reminds them that their way of thinking, relating, solving and being is wrong, or at least less than *right*.

A few neuroscientists believe that there is a precise location in the brain that is the seed of hand preference. However, they have not yet discovered its location. It is believed that some people become left-handed because of subtle injuries or lack of oxygen during the gestation period. These injuries are believed to knock out the area of the brain that governs dominance. This causes a switch of dominance to the other side.

It is also interesting to note that recent tests have shown that there is a link between the hand position of a left-handed writer and the placement of the language center in the brain. Sixty percent of the left-handers who arch their wrists above the line upon which they write have the language center in the left brain. The other 40 percent who write with their hands below the line (similar in manner to right-handers) were found to have language centers in the right or opposite brains. It is still unclear what the interrelationship is between the placement of the language center, specific language skills and the use of the hands. However, it is known that the language centers of right-handers are invariably on the left side of the brain.

Hand Specific. This is a category which describes people who use different hands for different activities. They change their hands at any given moment, not because of equal skill, but because of "lateral hesitancy" or doubt over which hand to use.

This hesitancy may lead to awkwardness or poor coordination, or both. Lack of a fixed preference in a hand can be quite a handicap. This is also called "mixed handedness" by some.

Ambidextrous. Ambidextrous means equally skilled in using both hands. A truly ambidextrous person is able to use either hand for any task as skillfully as he or she can use the other hand. There are few truly ambidextrous people, although Albert Einstein is an outstanding example of one who used both hemispheres and both hands to give *form* to *inspiration*. Most people thought to be ambidextrous are actually "hand specific" or have mixed hand dominance.

Mixed Hand Dominance. This describes the person who may use both hands for a variety of tasks, but the remainder are performed by one hand or the other. An example of this person is someone who always writes with his or her left hand, but may brush his or her teeth with either hand.

Test for Hand Dominance

There are several tests which can be given to determine the degree to which one hand is dominant. Generally, it is preferable to perform all three, since the combination of tests will provide the most accurate measurement of dominance.

Thumb Size. Check the size of your two thumbs. If you are right-handed your right thumb will be larger.

Split Fingers. Pair the second and third fingers and also the fourth and fifth fingers of both hands. Then stretch the paired fingers as far away from each other as possible. If the spaces between the paired fingers is greater in your left hand, you are right-handed.

Speech and Balance. Balance a dowel (or ruler, pen, etc.) on the index finger of your right hand and ask a friend to assist by timing the length of time you can balance it there *while talking*. Then transfer the dowel to the index finger of the opposite hand, following the same procedure. Note the difference between the two times.

Next, balance the dowel on the index finger of the right hand for as long as you can without talking. Have your friend time you. Repeat with the left hand, again noting the time.

A lower score for the right hand during the talking exercise means you are right-handed. Right-handers will score higher in the silent balancing exercise. Likewise, left-handers will score higher with their left hand in silence. Their right hand will score lower during the talking exercise.

Thumb Dominance

Clasp your hands tightly before you read further. Stop now and do this. Now read on—which thumb is on top?

Try another experiment before you read on. Clasp your hands so that the other thumb lands on top. Rate yourself as to whether it is just as easy to do as the first; a little more difficult; or nearly impossible.

Thumb dominance is very important in understanding "who is boss" in your personal system—the natural self or the ego self. The natural self has a will to express feeling and emotion and to recognize it in others. The ego's will is to achieve success in the objective world, gain respect and admiration from others, and accumulate material possessions.

In hand analysis, the thumb is considered the "will" of the personality. Many palmists believe it is the most important feature of the hand.

Which "will" is strongest in your personality? The natural feeling self of the left thumb, or the controlling ego of the right thumb?

The left thumb says, "I will to feel, to give love and get love. I am very sensitive to hostility and anger and I react strongly to threats to my personal integrity."

The right thumb says, "I will to rise in society, achieve goals and be in positions of authority and power. It is what I think that matters most. I want to be a rational, logical person, not given to impulsive and emotional behavior. I strive to be adult and serious."

The thumbs represent the two wills in the person. They can be in conflict or they can be complementary, as when both thumb positions feel comfortable with clasped hands. The other extreme occurs when one thumb is the controller, as evidenced by the great difficulty in allowing the non-dominant thumb to sit above the dominant thumb.

As we gain a more lucid understanding of ourselves through the exercises and readings of this book, it will become clear that a goal of balance between hemispheres, exemplified by the ambidextrous Einstein, is the lofty but preferable achievement for which we should strive. This becomes a state in which both hemispheres are equally active, inspired and innovative in translating ideas into fruition for the objective world to behold.

You can begin to move toward that ideal by working with your hand dominance. You can benefit by imaginatively exploring new uses for each of the hands. Try using the opposite hand for a typical action, like drawing, tracing or eating. Experience what it feels like.

By using your non-dominant hand, you stimulate the opposite hemisphere of the brain and increase your capacity for those potentials associated with it. You can further increase stimulation of that hemisphere by exercising and massaging your non-dominant hand. Each of us could probably use more balance in our lives.

3

Hands: Flesh and Skin

Those connected with the health profession are liable to make a number of observations, conduct several tests and record various data, before determining the state of your health. The same applies to hand analysis, which relies on certain observations and measurements weighed against each other to provide the most accurate indications of individual tendencies.

When analyzing a pair of hands, first make general observations about their shape and feel. Look at and touch your own. Do they feel soft or hard; firm or flabby; elastic or springy? Are they usually cold or warm? Are they often wet or dry?

Just as the look and color of your facial complexion indicates certain aspects of your health, so do your hands. Are your hands pink in color or do they lack luster and appear more white or grey?

After you've made those observations, press your thumb into the center of the opposite palm, placing your fingers on the back of that hand. Is the area thick or thin? Is there a hollow to your hand or does the palm have a flat center?

Record your observations on the following chart. It will provide a general backdrop against which to continue your examination of the hands. Remember, these observations alone will not provide a complete picture of you or the individual you are examining. However, these first impressions will provide indications of general tendencies.

FEEL				HAND COLOR		SKIN TEXTURE	
Soft	☐	Hard	☐	Pink	☐	Rough	☐
Firm	☐	Flabby	☐	Pale Pink	☐	Smooth	☐
Thick	☐	Thin	☐	Red	☐	Extra Smooth	☐

Flat	☐	Hollow	☐	Bluish	☐
Warm	☐	Cold	☐	White	☐
Wet	☐	Dry	☐	Black or Grey	☐
				Yellow	☐
				Ruddy	☐

Observations by hand analysts through the ages have shown close correlations between certain characteristics of the hands and certain personality traits. If you have firm, elastic, springy hands, you have abundant energy and are active in all ways. There is a "firmness" about your personality, yet a "flexibility" reflected in all that you do.

Very firm, but less elastic and springy hands probably indicate you are the kind of person who relies on force and strength. You don't really like soft-handed people for you feel that they are easily dominated.

If you have a soft hand, you are compassionate and sympathetic toward others; the perfect example of one who possesses the "milk of human kindness." Your imagination is more active than your intellect and you tend toward artistic, poetic or musical pursuits. Others find you easy to live with and love, because of your warm expressive nature. You are very flexible and adapt readily to whatever changing conditions you find around you. You can achieve through manipulation what others achieve by force. You tend to believe that hard-handed people are brutal and insensitive.

If your hands are soft and feel boneless, you may often lack the desire to act. If they are thick, soft and flabby, you seem unable to act, and dream instead. You have the potential for action, but may not snap out of your lethargy often. You can be indifferent to the needs of others, being wrapped up in your own concerns.

If your hands are thick and soft without being flabby, you may lack stamina. You can improve your personality by trying to broaden your outlook and you should try to improve your health. Your self-indulgence may have left you lazy, although you have a good imagination. With a little zest and zeal you could easily become an artist, poet or musician.

Thin soft hands indicate a person who is physically weak. If the thin hands are very, very soft, you may become very depressed. But in this case too, your hands can be the clue that tells you to improve your health. On the up side, you may be very intuitive, but should be careful about your temper.

If your hands appear swollen, it indicates you lack energy or that you may have liver trouble. Because of your lethargy, you appear indifferent. This may cause you to be moody and temperamental. Your satiric humor may cause you to lose friends and you should be extremely careful about offending others. You also may tend to be very conservative.

If you have thick hard hands, you are industrious, practical, steadfast and reliable. These "hardy" hands denote a hard worker. Reason prevails in your decision-making rather than emotions. In addition, if you have square-type palms, it is likely that you are a particularly good friend because of your sense of loyalty and sensible attitude. If your hands are very hard, you may be unreceptive to others. You may also repress your feelings. Sometimes hard hands are the result of manual labor, and this condition, which is not the result of a natural process, should be taken in to account.

Thick hands (as measured by the palm to the back of the hand) indicate a personality type who could easily oppress others in a desire to dominate them. Again, this is a trait that should be controlled.

If you find the flesh between the palm and back of the hand is so thin that the thumb and forefinger nearly touch, you may lack energy and a strong constitution. You should stretch your perspective and broaden your outlook. You should also overcome any tendencies to let others do what you should do for yourself.

Have you ever nervously anticipated an upcoming examination, walking into the classroom with butterflies in your stomach and wet, clammy hands? For some of us, that physical and emotional state is experienced infrequently. However, for others, wet palms are a common occurence.

It is your desire to do your best that often brings on the anxiety, and the sweaty palms. If your hands are wet most of the time, it means you are a hard worker; you are industrious and conscientious. You tend to overcome obstacles and face challenges with enthusiasm. You are a vital, warm-blooded and optimistic person who is very active physically. Your optimism includes positive feelings toward those around you.

If your hands are *always* perspiring, you are a lover of sensual experiences and enjoy luxury. You may even favor idleness to activity. Alternatively, if your hands tend to be cold and clammy, this condition may indicate signs of liver or other health problems.

There are those who seldom get rattled by any circumstances; who always seem in control of the situation. These individuals' emotions are well in check, as are the sweat glands in their hands. Their dry hands indicate that they are practical and even-tempered. If you have dry hands, you may appear unemotional to others, but you merely keep your feelings under control. However, this repression of feelings may lead to a variety of skin diseases that are psychosomatic in origin. You may also be vulnerable to fever as well.

The old saying, "warm hands, warm heart" is rooted in truth. Your warm hands indicate vitality—an outgoing, cheerful person ready to embrace life. You are "upbeat" and your positive emotions are expressed whenever the occasion warrants. Sometimes this tendency causes you to act impulsively and hastily. Your enthusiasm attracts others to you.

Extremely hot and dry hands indicate a fever. Hot and sweaty hands may be evidence of a hyperactive thyroid. In either case, medical attention is required.

Generally speaking, what warm hands have, cold hands lack. Cold hands indicate that you need more energy and may be weak physically. Your suspicious attitude toward others may cause you to become cold and calculating.

If your hands are cold and dry, an underactive thyroid gland may be in evidence. This may cause you to be self-indulgent and lacking in self-discipline. If this is the case, the fingers are usually sausage-shaped, with decidedly tapering fingertips and slow-growing nails.

In cases of acute shock, when blood pressure drops radically following a trauma, the hands become cold, clammy and bluish. But some of us are in a *mild* state of shock all the time, as seen in constantly cold and clammy hands (the color is normal). This condition suggests a chronically nervous person. People with cold wet hands travel in a constant state of anxiety.

Hand Color

Because our hands simultaneously reflect various conditions of our body's health, pink hands indicate the health that a pink facial complexion also represents. The person who has pink hands has a healthy blood circulation and tends to be filled with a sense of well-being and optimism. If you have pink hands, your sympathetic and compassionate nature helps you to relate well to others. Your gentleness and geniality illicits the trust of others; your confidence inspires the confidence of others in you.

Pale pink hand-coloration indicates that your personality is a bit colorless and you have a delicate constitution. You should have your blood content checked and use remedial means to improve circulation. Very pale hands are those of escapists who run away from trouble rather than face confrontation.

The enthusiasm associated with pink hands becomes passion in red hands. Crimson-colored hands denote an intense, passionate nature. You are driven by your passions, and may become impatient with others. You are such a "hard driver," you do not condone laziness of any kind. The red of your hands implies an increased supply of blood to the hands, and a body which thrives on the lifeblood of your passion. Beware, however, your zeal may lead to excesses in eating, drinking and other pursuits.

Ruddy hands are those of fighters. These are the hands of people who may easily lose their temper. If your hands are very red, you have a violent temper. You are also a candidate for high blood pressure.

If your hands are a dead-white color, you may be cold and lack enthusiasm. You may tend toward self-centeredness. This lack of coloration also indicates a lack of circulation and a deficiency in the blood.

Black or grey tints in your hands are often brought on by grief, sorrow or guilt. They may also indicate a variety of ailments including colic, bad lungs, heart trouble, liver disorder and dyspepsia. A visit to the physician would increase your chances for an improved lifestyle.

Bluish hands imply a pessimistic nature. These individuals may seek refuge from physical action, which is seen as futile. Their negative emotions may bring about a physical weakening of their own bodies. They are candidates for heart failure and other illnesses associated with poor circulation and sluggish blood.

If your hands are yellow, you tend to be morbid. You may also experience gastric distress caused by sluggishness of the liver or gall bladder.

Texture

The texture of the skin on the hands also helps to determine how a person will *feel* emotionally to us. How do you think you feel to others?

If you have rough skin, it is likely you have difficulty expressing yourself. Your constant chatter does little to reveal who you are. Because the real you is hidden, you often appear deceitful. However, you are a practical, solidly earthbound person who is essentially inartistic. You should leave creative pursuits to others who are less solidly planted on earth.

Hands with smooth, satiny skin are a pleasure to touch. They indicate a strong sense of aesthetics and possibly creative talent. This kind of skin usually belongs to a sensitive person. You are very aware of the textures you touch and conscious of the textures you see. In addition, your sensitivity to heat and cold may increase your vulnerability to rheumatism.

Extra-smooth skin has a fine silky feel and belongs to those whose sense of touch is exceptionally keen. This highly developed sense of touch encourages sensuality and a love for the feel of fine things. This person is often a "smooth talker" who loves self-adornment and impresses others with their ability to inspire confidence.

The most minute details of the hands carry their own significance and suggest certain characteristics about the personality. The hair color, lack or abundance of hair, as well as the area of the hand where it is found, also carry certain implications.

If you have very little hair, you are probably cautious and self-possessed, but energetic. If you are very hairy, you are intense by nature and excessively energetic. If you totally lack hair, you are likely to be refined, cultured and lacking in intense vigor.

If your hair color is light, you lack passion and are probably very suggestible. Likewise, if you have dark hair, you have an intense disposition and are quick to respond. Red hair denotes an excitable, tempestuous person.

Hair found only on the thumb means you are an inventive genius. Hair growing only on the lower two phalanges denotes a shy, awkward, stiff and self-conscious individual. Hair growing on all phalanges indicates an ardent nature that is easily aroused.

Remember when you checked the hollow of your palm by pressing the thumb and finger on either side of the hand? If you found the hollow of your palm flat but high (level with the mounts under the fingers) you are very proud, but your ego can lead to flareups of your violent temper. If the hollow is flat but low, you are timid and set very low goals in life. You need to develop more courage.

A moderately hollow palm is normal and does not imply any particular outstanding characteristics. A very hollow palm denotes a person who has difficulty keeping money and achieving success.

4

Hand Size

For centuries, hands have been used as a standard of measure roughly equal to four inches. To this day, hands are still used to specify the height of a horse. However, hand sizes are not standard. They vary greatly among individuals. Hands not only grow to different lengths and widths, but they are often mismatched to the bodies' size and stature. For this reason, many believe hand size carries its own significance, which can be used to "measure" individual tendencies.

Each one of us can be categorized as having small, medium or large hands. Each type, like the endomorph, ectomorph and mesomorph categories of body type, can be said to possess particular qualities. By learning our type, we can understand our own behavior and make greater use of our potential.

Test yourself, simply by lifting your hand up, palm toward your face. Place your chin into the hollow where your palm ends and wrist begins. Roll the surface of your palm against your nose and upward, touching your face, with your fingertips resting on your forehead.

If your fingertips touch your hairline or are close to it, you have large hands. If you are touching your eyebrows, you have small hands. If the tips of your fingers extend to the middle of your forehead, you have medium-sized hands.

If you have standard-sized hands, characteristics associated with both large and small hands will apply to you, only to a lesser degree. You will find you share tendencies attached to both sizes and can use all of their capacities. During the exercise, if you found your fingertips stretched closer to either the eyebrow or hairline, you may have stronger tendencies in that respective category.

Small Hands

Small-handed people have a tremendous drive to conquer, to reach the top of the heap, to achieve long-range goals. They seem to be a bundle of contained energy, moving forward with great power, single-mindedly pursuing one great goal. They aim high and far, marching ahead with speed and direction toward ambitious goals. For their size, they have far more energy than others. This gives them the momentum and confidence to succeed in whatever they do.

Small hands do not necessarily grow in proportion to a small body, though. Small hands can be found on large bodies and vice versa. The size of the hands is relative to brain size. For example, some individuals, particularly twins, are born with one hand smaller than the other. In such a case, the brain hemisphere governing that side will be smaller, and therefore, less dominant.

Small-handed people are extremely ambitious and real go-getters. Because they like large goals, but dislike petty details, they prefer to be the head of a project rather than the "go-fer." A small-handed person may say, "I think BIG, not small." In their attraction to the big scheme, the ambitious endeavor, they may become unscrupulous. They may even waste time daydreaming about their glories. Small-handed people are very intense and generally ego-directed, using reason and intellect rather than intuition.

If you have small hands, you function optimally when you have a goal in mind, regardless of its worth. You often want to save the world! You are considered a crusader, but are viewed as a fanatic if society disapproves of your goals.

Sometimes, you may be seen as unfriendly and incapable of relaxed social interaction, but that perspective is really unfair. Instead, you are intense and concentrate a lot of power in a small space.

Medium Hands

If your hands rest in the middle of your forehead, you have an even, cool temperament and are able to deal with both large- and small-handed people. In fact, you may often act as a mediator between them! You are balanced and your judgment is good. You share in moderation all the traits associated with both types of hands, yet you are generally able to eliminate their negative traits and integrate more positive ones into your personality. You have a lot of common sense and practicality, as well as a moderate, healthy imagination. You can find out quite a bit about your personality by reading the descriptions of small- and large-handed people and moderating the descriptions of their traits.

Large Hands

Large hands indicate a person who is versatile and many-sided. While a small-handed person is characterized by the power of single-minded concentration, the lifestyle of the large-handed person is often that of diffused energy, which has a wide pattern but lacks deep penetration.

You are capable of pursuing different goals simultaneously, perhaps by holding down more than one job at a time. You are able to succeed at each pursuit. You often have varied talents, and like to develop all of them in one lifetime. You move slowly but broadly through life, in contrast to the speedy, narrow journey of small-handed people. You have the capacity to channel energy in differing directions at the same time. You prefer short-term goals and encompass many small successes.

The framework of your life can contain a variety of skills and abilities, all operating at the same time. A good example of a large-handed person is a psychologist I know. He teaches a full load of classes, takes duty in the university infirmary as a full-time member of the staff, and is deeply engrossed in an important research project. In addition, he is intently pursuing a line of study for his own personal growth. Yet, despite all this movement, his plans for the future do not extend beyond the next two to three years.

If you have large hands, you are immediately friendly and sociable in your interactions with others because you are interested in a variety of areas, and you like so many kinds of people! You like to talk, tell jokes and emphasize the less serious side of life. You seem less selfish than those with small hands, but this is not so. You are just as intent in accomplishing your many goals as the small-handed person is in accomplishing the more singular achievements. Because you reject far-reaching goals, you may spread yourself too thin. Your horizons are limited because of your lack of compulsion to seek out "greatness." Instead, you will live in a world of casual accomplishment.

Which type are you? How well are you matched with those you encounter around you? If you find yourself mismatched with a friend, spouse, partner or even parent, this may be one possible source of conflict. These insights may help you to bridge the chasm of the two types.

The length of the hand is only one of the measurements used to indicate certain personality traits. While size is very important, it is not the only indicator of personality. With other characteristics, it must be weighed, balanced and synthesized to present a true picture of all your character traits.

It is possible to discover other specific traits by measuring the lengths of the fingers and the back of the hand, as well as the width of the palm. The length of the fingers are gauged in relation to the measurement of the back of the hand.

Hold your hands up sideways, in the position illustrated below. Measure from the wrist bone, which lies on top of the curved wrist, to the top of the knuckle of the middle finger. Then measure from the same knuckle tip to the tip of the middle finger. Although your eye may be sufficient to estimate, the measurements are easy to do with a ruler and far more accurate.

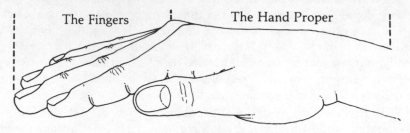

The Fingers   The Hand Proper

Figure 4-1. Measuring the Fingers and Hand

If the fingers measure shorter than the back of the hand, you are a short-fingered type. If the fingers are longer, you belong to the long-fingered category. If the measurements are the same, you share the characteristics of both types.

There is much variation within these types and many different comparative lengths. By observing your friends, you can learn some of the subtle disparities. In my own experience, I have also found that people with each of the three types of finger-lengths tend to associate with other people who have similar finger-lengths.

In a simple natural setting, such as the ones where more primitive cultures thrive, long fingers have enabled group members to be sensitive to changes in nature and climate, other animate life surrounding them, as well as the activity below the earth. One reason for this is because longer fingers contain more receptor cells (cells that transmit touch) and therefore intensify the sensitivity of the hands.

Thus, the longer the fingers are, the more sensitivity the person has to the environment. When the environment poses great threat to the physical survival of the individual, then longer fingers are helpful. However, in a complex, urban society, long sensitive fingers can be stress receptors as they perceive the conflicts and contradictions around them. As civilization developed, the cooperation of larger and larger groups ensured protection and survival. Thus the need for longer fingers lessened.

Short Fingers

If you have short fingers, you are a holistic thinker who grasps a situation with quick understanding. You are able to synthesize well and are intuitive if your fingers are smooth (not gnarled or knotty). You are impulsive and action-oriented, and the shorter your fingers are, the more impatient you can be. You may also be shallow, preferring to skim the surface of life rather than diving into its depths. Because you are more oriented to physical action, rather than mental action, you may have a reputation as a go-getter.

Below are examples of what different types of fingertips will mean to people with short fingers:

Figure 4-2. Pointed Fingertip

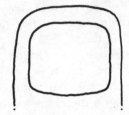

Figure 4-3. Square Fingertip

People with pointed fingertips may be lazy dreamers (see Figure 4-2).

People with square tips have a useful hand and are reliable employees (see Figure 4-3).

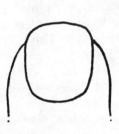

Figure 4-4. Conical Fingertip

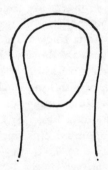

Figure 4-5. Spatulate Fingertip

People with conical tips would make talented artists. They are rather sensuous (see Figure 4-4).

People with spatulate tips love sports and all physical activity (see Figure 4-5).

If you have a wide palm, you like action with no delay! If, however, you are short-fingered with a narrow palm, you are spontaneous and enjoy change in your physical and social surroundings.

Extremely short fingers indicate laziness and indifference. Your primitive instincts are strong and you are most impulsive. In addition, very short-fingered people are unconventional and lack economic common sense.

Those with short fingers will find themselves to be incompatible with long-fingered people, who tend to be deep thinkers and slow workers.

Long Fingers

People with long fingers are highly sensitive to their environment. They are thoughtful, civilized and artistic. They also have a great aptitude for doing small projects well because they love detail. These people are analytical and methodical with a good memory, but lack broad vision. Long-fingered people don't like to depend on others, but actually prefer that others rely on them. They work best when they work slowly and tend to procrastinate taking action. In fact, they have a hard time keeping up with the action surrounding them.

The longer your fingers are in relation to the palm, the greater the empathy you feel to other living things. In a discordant and harsh environment, this sensitivity to others can cause you to undergo intense pain and suffering. This awareness of the pain of others will undoubtedly increase your own level of stress and tension.

Unlike very short-fingered people, long-fingered individuals are very much tuned in to discord in the world. Those with short fingers may even create the conflict, in their fight for what they want. Likewise, long-fingered people often will create the movement toward an atmosphere of accord and harmony which others may enjoy.

If your fingers are exceptionally long, you are a meddler and fault-finder in other's lives. A predisposition to deception or diplomacy will be evident if your fingers are long and thin. The most patient of all long-fingered types are those with wide palms and large nails. This type is well-suited to the profession of scientific research. However, if you measure a narrow palm with long fingers, this person tends to delay.

Below are examples of what different types of fingertips will mean to people with long fingers:

With pointed tips, you are idealistic, imaginative, impulsive and intuitive. There is a healthy flow of energy between you and the environment (see Figure 4-2).

With square tips, you are a hard worker with an acumen for business. You are attentive to detail and therefore difficult to decieve. You are a deliberate, decisive individual who thinks through everything thoroughly before making decisions (see Figure 4-3).

With conical tips, imagination and practicality work together well. The cogs of the wheels of inspiration and execution rotate in unison. You have clear, rapid insight into others and quick comprehension of detail. This type of fingertip is often found on the hands of musicians, composers or actors (see Figure 4-4).

With spatulate tips, it is likely that you are very active, but get bogged down with detail. Outdoor sports and travel attract your energetic and adventurous nature. You are versatile with a good sense of humor (see Figure 4-5).

Palm Size

In general, men's palms are wider than women's and are associated with what are traditionally thought of as "male qualities." Likewise, a narrow palm usually indicates characteristics which are traditionally considered feminine.

You can determine your palm size by measuring the width of your hand. If that measurement exceeds the length of the hand proper (measured from knuckle to wrist), you have wide palms. If the width is less than the length, you have narrow palms. However, if they are equal, you have square palms.

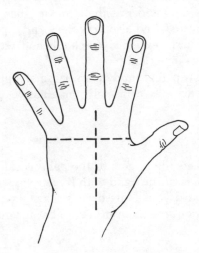

Figure 4-6. Determining Palm Size

Those with wide palms are direct, definite, abrupt, vigorous, confident and secure in fields of action. They perform tasks with a minimum of effort. Wide palms usually have well-developed mounts, which indicate good health and a balanced temperament. However, very wide palms found on thick hands denote an excessive imagination, aggressiveness and tendencies toward deception. A wide and very flat palm generally belongs to those who are more intellectual and less physical in their expression.

While those with wide palms will move directly into the action of life, those with narrow palms tend to be more manipulative. They tend to act more indirectly on the environment and may extend maximum effort before anything is accomplished. Planning, organizing and delegating authority are some of their strongest abilities, although they may feel insecure in areas where aggressive action is required to produce results.

Narrow-palmed people may be very mercurial. They may also be inclined to pessimism. Narrow palms physically lack the room for a well-developed mount of imagination, so those possessing narrow palms may be inclined to be more pragmatic. When faced with a conflict, they may prefer a more retiring stance, rather than an act of bravery.

People with square palms, however, love action. They prefer mobility and are generally greatly attracted to physical activity.

Square hands with short fingers indicate a practical person who is dependable and reliable. Those with square hands with long fingers tend to be cheerful, extroverted and ambitious. These people strive for intellectual growth.

Wide palms are rarely found, but when seen, they speak of an individual who is concerned only with satisfying basic, physical needs.

A narrow or oblong palm indicates an emotionally sensitive person. The person is introverted if the palm is wider at the bottom than at the top. If, however, the palm is wider at the knuckles than toward the wrist, the individual is extroverted, and also very fiery and expressive. This person is very intuitive and can be extremely excitable and active. These individuals express their feelings in action.

The very narrow palm found on a very small hand indicates a sensitive withdrawn person who is extremely imaginative, but does not express it in action.

Finger Cast-Off

The line that connects the fingers to the palm is called the finger cast-off. Look at the underside of the hand with fingers spread slightly. Move your fingers slightly toward you. Now draw an imaginary line below the four fingers where they join the palm proper. That is your finger cast-off.

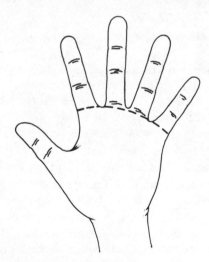

Figure 4-7. Finger Cast-Off

Match your imaginary line with the following cast-off lines.

Figure 4-8. Tudor Arch

Figure 4-8 is called the Tudor Arch and it is a line that runs evenly across the hand. A strong equal base for all your fingers, it indicates self-confidence, assurance, aggressiveness and drive. These people can trust their own judgment. They have a tendency, though, to be fixed.

Figure 4-9. Norman Arch

Figure 4-10. Perpendicular Arch

Figure 4-9 is called the Norman Arch; it is also the "norm." The line extends evenly with a slight drop beneath the index finger and little finger. This line is average, healthy and normal.

Figure 4-10 is called the Perpendicular Arch, with a low-set index and little finger. Such a type would be inclined to feel inferior, with little self-appreciation.

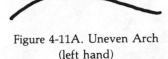

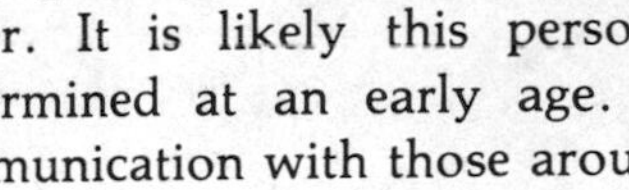

Figure 4-11A. Uneven Arch
(left hand)

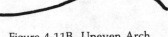

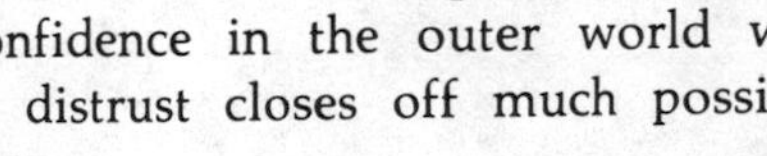

Figure 4-11B. Uneven Arch
(right hand)

Figures 4-11A–B are uneven arches. These lines droop off at the little finger. It is likely this person's confidence in the outer world was undermined at an early age. Their distrust closes off much possible communication with those around them.

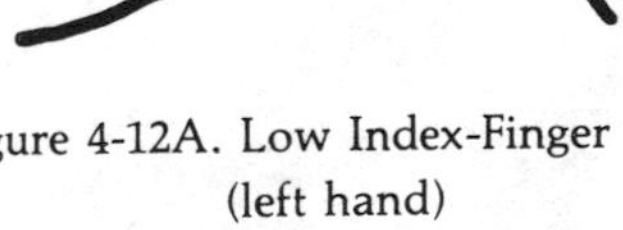

Figure 4-12A. Low Index-Finger Arch
(left hand)

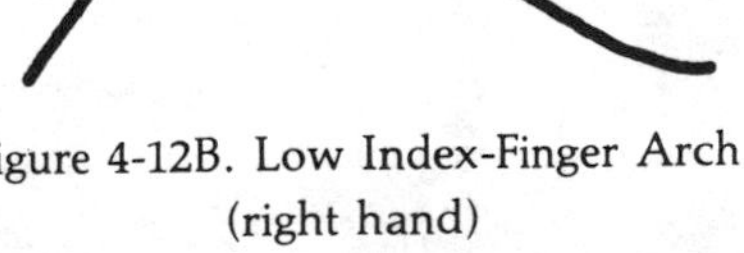

Figure 4-12B. Low Index-Finger Arch
(right hand)

In Figures 4-12A–B, the index fingers are placed in a low position, representing lack of self-confidence. A severe inferiority complex is indicated, as well as great dependence on others. This situation continues to fuel feelings of helplessness and powerlessness.

5

The Major and Minor
Classifications of the Hand

Now that we have thoroughly examined the size and shape of the palm and fingers, you can easily find your Major Hand Classification. By examining your own hands you can know the ways in which you can find satisfaction and fulfillment in this lifetime. We each arrive on this earth with all the natural inclinations to develop ourselves. We grow from infants, developing our bodies and minds. Throughout this development our bodies "mirror" the growth of our inner selves as they take on bulk and shape. Therefore, many of your "natural inclinations" are revealed by the bulk and shape of your hands.

The hand-type classification describes a "class," a combination of individual characteristics combined to make a whole group. Although there is variety within a particular class, especially of degree, the class does impose a certain structure. Therefore, it may be possible to live outside your "class"; however, choosing a lifestyle which is a natural extension of your group will help assure that you use your own distinctive form of being to its best advantage. Certain hand types are suited for particular vocations or aspirations; each has a contribution to make to society and to the self within. If you are working within your hand class, you will be far more successful and happy.

These are the major hand types:

Elementary. Coarse skin, thick flesh, heavy palm, short fat fingers. The palm bones form almost the whole hand so that it has more palm than fingers. These short-fingered, thick-handed people are here to experience the basic physical existence. They need to learn skills of a physical nature and how to handle their instinctive nature in positive ways.

These people work very hard, as these hands are usually accompanied by a powerful physique. They also make good fighters, for their insensitivity to pain is the greatest of all hand types. It parallels their insensitivity to the pain of others, and so to evolve, they must learn to become more sensitive and helpful.

That combination of insensitivity and brute strength predisposes them to be forceful and sometimes even violent. They often use physical strength to get what is desired. However, they are extremely loyal to those who show them kindness and tolerance, for although they are not intellectuals, they have a native intelligence that is aware of others' attitudes and feelings in a very basic way.

Their feeling nature is not highly developed and they can appear completely unemotional. They are stoics, enduring great privations and pain with little complaint. If they are ill-treated under those conditions, their reaction may be brutish, and they may be inclined to cause great harm to their tormentor.

Practical. Also called the square hand because the palm is square; the width at the wrist is equal to the width of the knuckles. Also, the fingers are equal in length to the hand proper. Closed together, the fingers form another square.

This square-type hand belongs to individuals who may once have been called "square." They are orderly, punctual, precise and duty-disciplined workers. They conform to habit and have a high regard for authority figures. They are here to experience working with, and particularly for, other people. They love to work and are very conservative, even tradition-bound. These people extoll the virtues of social customs and traditions to such a degree that they will dispute any who exhibit non-conformity. They fight fiercely for their own rights. These types may have a predisposition to become members of organizations such as the Moral Majority, the conservative, right-wing group known for its support of family life and the puritan work ethic.

Because they are so down-to-earth, those with practical hands are also known as earth types. Inclined to be self-centered, they worship money and status. They are often successful in the material world because they are willing to forego short-term gratification for future gains. They are also devoted family members.

They are strong-willed, stubborn and forceful of character. They are fervent in their perseverance, particularly in conforming to law and convention.

These conscientious workers like precision and order on the job. Members of this group usually have blunt fingers and squarish nails and are frequently employed in the business sector.

Imaginative. Also called the Conic Hand. This hand is oblong in shape with straight tapering fingers that have oval tips. When closed, this hand is narrow where the fingertips meet, swelling outward like a teardrop and ending at the wrist. The fingers rise smooth from their base, getting narrower at the tips.

Intuition and imagination are strong themes in the lives of this group. In fact, their vivid imagination and great enthusiasm is so dominant, it sparks their impulsivity and often gets them into trouble. They are charming and convivial; however, when discouraged, they are apt to sink into deep chasms of despair. The acting profession and musical realm are well populated with this type of person. They adore beautiful surroundings and furnish their homes attractively. Their aesthetic sense is very strong; they seek luxury and beauty in their environment.

They are not suited to the practical business world because of their impulsivity. They are great theorizers and apt visionary planners. They are inspirational and instinctive. Imaginative-type people, they are entertaining conversationalists, easy to know and intriguing. They generally make favorable impressions on others.

However, they are very mercurial, sentimental, moody and temperamental. Their romantic sense of life propels them to continually seek change and variety. They tend to be extremists in their ideas, opinions, likes and dislikes. They make exceptional revolutionaries and are emotional leaders. Their best qualities may emerge when they are subjected to firm discipline.

Psychic. An exaggerated version of the Conic, except the fingers are slim, smooth and straight.

These people possess all the qualities of the imaginative type, and *more!* The intuitive skills of the imaginative type are further sharpened and become psychic in this type. The long slender fingers of the psychic type make them sensitive not only to this world, but to other worlds of knowledge as well. The result is that these people are more interested in developing psychic skills than applying themselves to the mundane business of earning a living or dealing with practical matters.

Their psychic pursuits may lead them on a path of alienation, away from conventional people. But these people create their own group, usually by seeking out each other. They are idealistic, ardent and intense. They tend to be volatile if their "world view" is challenged.

Sensitive. A rectangular palm forming an oblong shape that is quite narrow.

There are three categories within this classification: flat-topped, squared fingertips; pointed fingertips; and almond-shaped fingernails on a long, fragile hand. All three types are here to experience their own sensitivity and move from self-centeredness outward toward awareness of others' feelings.

All three types are typically women, and most often these women possess great beauty and sex appeal. These are the hands that belong to models, actresses and performers of all types. Their need for attention is very great and admiration is the recognition they crave. They tend to look toward others for material and emotional support.

These are the characteristics of each of the subcategories:

Sensitive Square Fingertips. This category of people tends to be very egotistical and desirous of accumulating wordly goods. They have a tendency to see the negative aspects of life since they experience their own hurts or slights in exaggeration. The result is a pessimistic, despondent nature. If these people lack the admiration or love they seek, they may use material luxuries and riches to compensate.

They are often so sensitive themselves they cannot perceive the sensitivities of others. This group needs to develop their compassion for others and an awareness of the natural beauty in the world around them. They can learn to merit love and affection by giving first and responding to others' needs.

Sensitive Pointed Fingertips. These individuals certainly possess a rare type of hand. Their sensitivity is greatly accentuated. Fond of color and music, they are greatly affected by both. Their sensitive nature lends to an emotional personality. Many are difficult individuals to understand and hard to satisfy. They often seek satisfaction in religious expression. Those with pointed fingertips seem to penetrate higher realms of thought in a mystical way. They tend to retreat from the world unless there is an opportunity to shape the world in their way.

Sensitive Almond-Shaped Fingernails on Conical Fingertips. This type of person lacks energy. Usually very beautiful, these people are emotionally very intense. They are vulnerable in the heart and lung area and should watch for indications of heart and lung problems. These nails can also curve like claws, and "catty" behavior can overshadow this type of individual's strengths.

Usually these people are idealistic and very spiritual. They are inspired by beauty, peace and tranquility. They are quiet and gentle, confident and trustworthy. Honest and openly innocent, they prove quite impractical in the everyday world. They seek to surround themselves with music, color, dancing. If spiritual, they continually desire the truth—their capacity for mystery is deep and their curiosity is great. They sense the majesty of life, which attracts them to delve further into many areas of the unknown.

Acting as mediums, clairvoyants and spiritists attracts them. Imbued with highly developed ESP skills, their precognitive visions are often accurate. However, they can become morose, melancholy and morbid. They need much nurturing from others, because they are quite helpless to cope with the practical world.

Philosophic. An angular-shaped hand with long palms and long fingers that have knotty, bumpy-looking finger joints. Fingers tend to be very firm and long with long, squarish nails.

This angular hand-type indicates a searching, analytical mind. These people are continually weighing questions, sifting facts and searching for the truth. The knots in the finger joints indicate a desire for wisdom. This inquiring mind is often found in teachers, philosophers or scientists.

Independent, they prefer to do their own research and reach their own conclusions. They seek to illuminate truth rather than covet material possessions or money. They are drawn to the mysterious, the dark side of life. Don't be fooled by their silence or secretiveness, for they are idealistic and ambitious concerning their goals.

They are successful in their pursuits because of their ability to submerge themselves in the abstract. However, this gift leaves them quite impractical in other concerns, much like the absent-minded professor. Their fuel on earth is their sense of purpose, which drives them to discover the meaning of all things and the reason why they are here.

These individuals are well suited to becoming hypnotists, mystics, yogis, saints, reformers, psychics. They are often mind-readers, with plenty of ESP power. We also find them among the preachers, teachers and psychiatrists of the world. However, if the entire hand has become misshapen, it indicates the person has lost the innocence of a purpose on earth and has become critical and cynical instead.

Spatulate. Also known as the Energetic hand type. The fingertips are wide at the top and narrow just below the top, forming a "waist." The thumbs are usually large and the wrist broad. The base of the fingers tends to be wide also.

These people are physically very active with an abundance of motivation. They may, however, become restless if there is no outlet available for their energies. Very independent, they resent interference in their affairs. Handle them with respect and tact, for they are our pioneers.

These individuals live to create order out of chaos, construct organization where none exists, or fill empty space with objective form. They can be, for example, the architects who view an empty plot of land and envision the building that can be constructed there. They are propelled into unknown spaces and undeveloped places. Whether that be a wilderness forest or a new scientific paradigm. They love adventure!

With their vast energy and enthusiasm, they are willing to tackle the "impossible dream," and breathe life into form. Their power of imagination is so robust, they can perceive what could be, how it would be, and what it takes to make it be. They bring to fruition the results of their fertile imagination.

Some are interior designers who look at empty rooms and visualize the combination of furnishings that will make an artistic form. This feeling of aesthetic harmony draws some of this group into the field of art, where an empty canvas is a challenge. These people are able to transform inner images outward, through their skillful fingers.

Mixed Hand Type. This hand type is a composite of any other types. This allows greater versatility for these individuals. The mixed hand type has a variety of ideas and is readily adaptable to changing purposes and circumstances. They borrow ideas freely from others, adopting others' thoughts and feelings as their own.

However, these people are usually original thinkers, combining ideas in innovative ways. They generally improve on whatever thoughts they borrow from others. They can bring ideas to life, in countless ways. They are also tactful, diplomatic, friendly and gregarious.

They are so attracted to action and adventure, some take years to finally settle down to one occupation, while others never do. Their versatility predisposes them to be restless and even volatile.

As actors or actresses, they can take on many roles of very different dimensions and play each one authentically. They are quite capable of showing different sides of themselves to different people.

The Minor Classifications of the Hands

The four elements of fire, water, earth and air are used to describe the categories of hands based on an examination of the palmar lines. Palmar lines are the grooves of the hands commonly associated with palm readings. The three basic lines are the heart, head and life lines. They are diagrammed below.

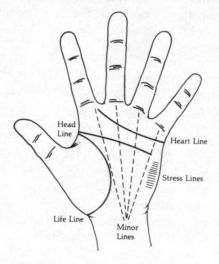

Figure 5-1. Major and Minor Lines

Look at your lines. Are they deep and wide? Or are they fine and faint? Are there many smaller lines all over the palm?

A second form of minor classification is based on categorizing types by examining the mounts of the hands. The seven mounts, found at various spots on the palm of the hand, are named after the planets: Jupiter, Apollo (Sun), Venus, Saturn, Mercury, Mars and Luna (Moon). Below is an illustration of the seven mounts found on the hands. You will fall into a particular planetary category if you have one mount which is noticeably higher, fatter and more densely colored than the rest of your palm.

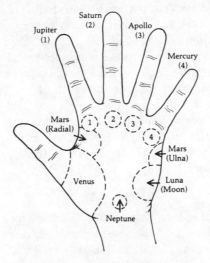

Figure 5-2. Plains and Mounts

Whenever there is a lot of activity in your life in an area represented by a particular mount, the blood vessels at that specific place will become enlarged. The enlarged blood vessels in turn trigger a protective response that causes the flesh over that area to become bulkier. These small areas of the palms correspond to areas in the brain where the hands have their neural connections.

The mounts, then, have a high color because of the relative amount of blood flow that is triggered by the parallel activity in the brain. We each choose the areas of our lives that we will invest our energy into, and these, in turn, develop our mounts. In reverse, we are able to now read the mounts to determine the areas into which we have devoted our energies. Some of these choices have been life-long endeavors, but some of us may want to change them. Knowledge of your present choices can assist you in increasing the powers associated with that particular mount, or expanding activity into new dimensions, thereby accentuating another mount.

When examining the palmar lines, it is possible to categorize the kinds of lines that appear into one of four classifications—Earth, Air, Fire and Water. If you consider that generally earth types are "down to earth"; air types are mentally adept; fire types are very volatile; and water types quite "soulful," then what type do you suspect you are? Read on and see.

Earth Type

The major lines (head, heart, and life lines) are usually deep and simply constructed in the earth hand. These hands are noted for the lack of minor lines and stress lines. There is no delicate network of fine lines and few minor lines can be found. The palm is always square, and the fingers are short or of the same length as the hand. (This hand is known as the practical or elemental type in the major classification system.)

The elemental hand usually has just three deeply engraved major lines. These people are very down-to-earth and physical in their expression. When the fingers are as long as the palm (practical type), the hand will show a few minor lines and perhaps some stress lines.

In general, earth types are practical, loyal and very hard workers. They may be dull companions, but they are steady and dependable when you need a friend. Once they have chosen a friend, their loyalty is undivided and unchangeable. They are just as fixed once they have chosen an enemy, as well.

Air Type

These hands must have long fingers to be classified as air types. Major lines are sometimes shallow and the sensitivity of these types brings on some fine-textured stress lines. This hand is usually well marked with minor lines. The head line is long, showing intellectuality.

Air-type people are "airy" and their heads are often in the clouds—out of the practical realm of ideas and thoughts. Mentally-oriented rather than emotional, they are the thinkers, the idea people, rather than ones who bring ideas to fruition.

Daydreaming and absent-mindedness are common in air types. They are introverted, quiet people and have minds seething with ideas. If their major lines are fine and shallow, they are easily startled and often brought down to earth with a bang by other people.

Fire Type

Fire types are indicated by deep obvious lines. In fact, there are more deep lines than faint ones. The major lines are deep and clearly seen. There are many minor lines which criss-cross the palmar area, indicating the outflow of strong energy.

This is an emotional type, fiery in nature. They are aggressive and usually very expressive of their feelings. Explosive tempers mark these people, yet their enthusiasm can be contagious. Their extroverted nature makes them good actors or leaders of emotionally-based causes. They lavish affection on others.

These kinds of linear markings are usually found on a hand where the base of the palm is narrower than the width across the base of the fingers. The fingers have a wide spread and hand gesturing is common because their intensity of feeling is so great. Words alone do not suffice for them.

These people can be overpowering in their intense desire to give affection and receive attention. When aroused, their anger is as great as their love and they can steam up a water-type person into an explosion of seldom expressed emotion. The fire types can also arouse the placid earth types, but the most serious explosion occurs when the fire type antagonizes the air type. This is a combustion of airy ideas and fiery beliefs.

Occasionally, square hands also have fire lines, but this type is calmer, less volatile and more introverted. Even so, their feelings give great power to their actions and words.

Fire types are as unbendable as their passions are deep. They are optimistic, dramatic, explosive and volatile. Truly, they are very spirited people.

Water Type

These hands indicate a very emotional person with extremely fine lines criss-crossing the major lines, which are also narrow and fine. Water types are high-strung and very nervous. They are sensitive to their environment and, like water, are a fine conductor of electrical energy. They can absorb tremendous amounts of energy from others and are inclined to be pessimistic when they are denied attention and affection.

Sentimental and very receptive, they love to have their birthdays remembered and to receive loving attention. They withdraw easily when their feelings are threatened and avoid or run away from confrontation, rather than fight for their own rights.

The webbed effect of all the fine lines indicates an extremely active nervous system that constantly picks up "charges." Very reactive, they need a tremendous amount of affection and approval. If the lines are excessive, they are hypersensitive. They are the "soulful" types as opposed to the "spirited" fire types.

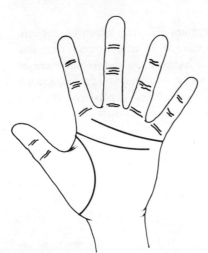

Figure 5-3. Earth Type

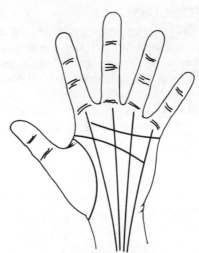

Figure 5-4. Fire Type

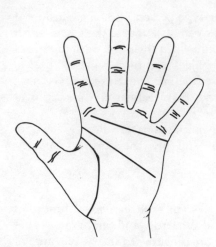

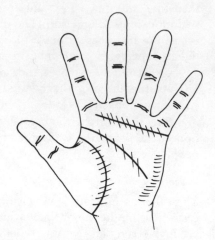

Figure 5-5. Air Type   Figure 5-6. Water Type

Planetary Minor Classifications

When considering the planetary minor classifications, it is important to remember that four of the mounts are Jupiter, Saturn, Apollo and Mercury. Before you decide your type, remember that the finger connected to one of those four mounts must be large and well-developed before it can be considered your true mount type.

Both hands must be equally developed before you can conclude that one of these is your type. If the hands differ in mount development, you should look to the later section on mounts to understand why.

Jupiterian Type

The index finger must be large and accompanied by an elevated mount. Very confident and jovial, these people exercise authority through personal magnetism. They expand themselves in whatever their interests are to become a leader to the rest, taking positions as executives or administrators. They can be "larger than life," as they are either egotistical or self-actualizers, depending on their orientation. They continually seek to improve their self-image or self-growth.

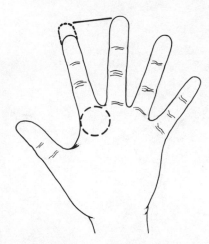
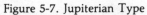
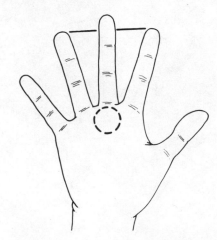

Figure 5-7. Jupiterian Type   Figure 5-8. Saturnian Type

Saturnian Type

They must also have a large middle finger, accompanying a high mount below. This type is uncommon. There is usually a hollow below the Saturn finger. Members of this group tend to be self-sacrificing and pessimistic. They are inclined toward the melancholy and are serious with a great sense of social obligation and duty toward others.

Apollonian Type

Happy individuals, they follow their own path and achieve success on it. Their sunny disposition brings them many friends. Their primary purpose is to express themselves in some area of society. Therefore, creative and artistic pursuits suit them well. The stage attracts many Apollonians and fame can be achieved because of their unique personal contributions to others.

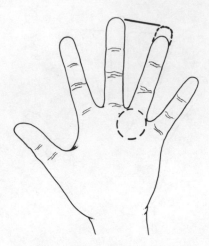
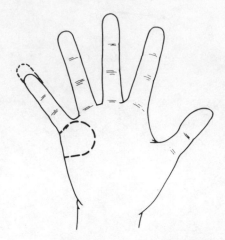

Figure 5-9. Apollonian Type   Figure 5-10. Mercurian Type

Mercurian Type

Like the mercury of the thermometer rising and falling with the weather, these people change frequently and are quite mutable. Generally, they are great communicators and glib talkers. Their ESP is well developed and they know quickly what others are thinking and feeling. Those insights help them to respond instantaneously.

Martian Type

Members of this group are always ready for a fight! If the three sections across the palm are all elevated, this person will tend to be aggressive, warlike and best suited for soldiering. If the thumb side is highly developed, they will love competition and will possess great moral resistance and courage if the ulna side is elevated. A hollow in the Plain of Mars subdues the warlike characteristics, emphasizing courage and bravery instead.

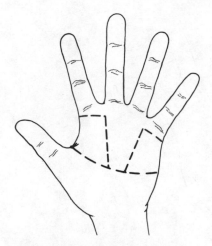

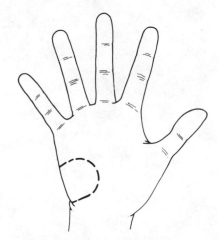

Figure 5-11. Martian Type   Figure 5-12. Lunar Type

Lunar Type

The lunar type probably has a vivid imagination. Redness in this area indicates an active unconscious mind. Inspired from the muse of their unconscious, they can visualize and organize spontaneous ideas into rational concepts. Because they frequently delve into the depths of their own unconscious, they may be skilled in "automatism," or psychic abilities such as automatic writing and dowsing.

Venusian Type

This kind of person is a great lover, desiring to put affection into action. They love physical activity and are inclined toward athletics. Many love sports and work at jobs requiring constant physical change and movement. They demonstrate a fondness for nature and animals. If their Mars mount is flat, they prefer solitary sports such as mountain climbing. However, if their Mars mount is well developed, they are excited by competitive sports.

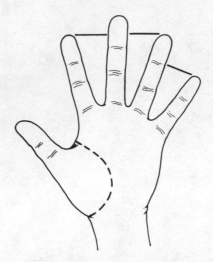

Figure 5-13. Venusian Type

In the next chapter, you will see how the manner in which your fingers grew shows your relationship with early life influences. You will learn how much "weight" your fingers had to bear and what that has to do with the development of your personality.

6

Finger Growth

Think of your hands as two trees, with your fingers as the branches. Any deviation in the straightness of the tree trunk or its branches is due to outside influences, pressures and circumstances; so it is with the hands and fingers. "As the tree is bent, the tree will grow" illustrates the principle of finger growth.

By their nature, hands grow straight out from the wrist and fingers extend directly from the hand. Any curving or bending of the skeletal part of the hand is caused by the outside pressures of life, the parents, family, society or experiences. Just as we can examine trees to find how the winds, storm and climates have affected their growth, so we can examine hands to detect the early influences in the life of the individual.

When a tree is stunted, it is from the tremendous pressure of great forces which prevented its growth. When any finger does not achieve its full growth, we know that powerful forces at work early in the environment prevented it from growing to its full potential. Likewise, when a finger experiences exceptional growth, we realize that optimum conditions for development were present in the early life, thereby encouraging and nurturing the individual.

Looking at the illustration of the skeleton of the hand in Figure 6-1, you can see the joints between the bones that become our knuckles when clothed with flesh. The palmar area includes the four metacarpal bones extended from each finger and the third phalange of the thumb. The different skeletal structure of the thumb, as opposed to the fingers, carries its own significance, so we will deal with thumbs specifically in a later chapter. The largest mount in area is the thumb, and therefore, the most important mount we have.

The illustration of the skeletal hand shows normal bone growth in an unwarped hand, and the length of the fingers is standard. How does your hand differ from the illustration?

Any deviation from the skeletal structure of the normal hand shown should be noted as a unique characteristic that you have developed during your lifetime of experiences. But in order to understand what effects the differences signify, we must examine each digit and the experiences associated with it.

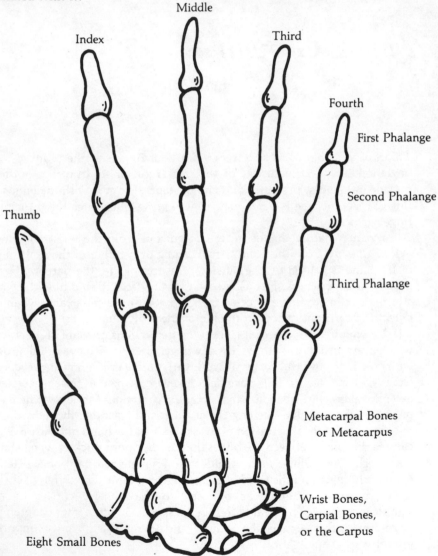

Figure 6-1. The Skeleton of the Hand

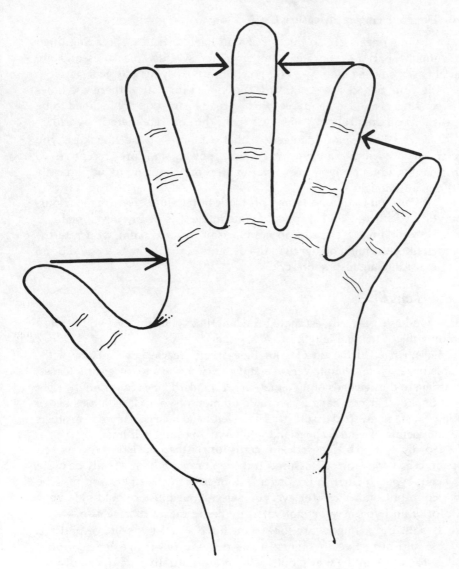

Figure 6-2. Normal Growth of the
Hand

Each finger is long or short in relationship to its own family of fingers. To measure your own, close up the fingers and thumbs on a flat surface. The norm is as follows: The thumb tip reaches to the middle of the first phalange of the index finger. The tip of the index finger reaches to the middle of the top phalange of the middle finger. The third finger is equal in length to the index finger. The little fingertip touches the crease line (or knob at the back of the hand) of the third phalange of the ring finger.

How Do Your Fingers "Measure Up"?

• If your fingers are so thick that you have difficulty spreading them far enough apart to separate them, you like worldly pleasures and are acutely aware of the messages you receive through your physical sense.

• If your fingers are so thin that in closed formation there are holes between fingers and larger spaces when spread apart, you are inclined to be idealistic. You are probably alienated from the concrete material world.

• If you have smooth fingers with no bumps at the knuckles, you prefer to use intuition over reasoning power and are receptive to information. If your fingers are smooth and short, you tend to judge hastily without forethought.

• If your joints are knotty and protrude at the sides, you are tenacious, analytical, deliberate and skeptical. Your intellect is highly developed.

• If your fingers are slim in comparison to your palm, you rate the enjoyment of the mind higher than the delights of the flesh. You could be an ascetic, leading an austere lifestyle.

Finger Length

Once you have generally estimated the length of your fingers, you need to examine the individual length of each finger.

Index Finger. If the tip of your index finger reached the middle of the middle finger, you are quite versatile and can either be a follower or a leader, according to the demands of the situation. A standard index finger on the right hand implies that you have a favorable opinion of yourself as a member of society. A standard-sized first finger on the left hand means that you feel others are considerate of your feelings and you have a positive self-image.

However, if your right index finger is longer than the left, it means you appear to be confident, self-assured and even brave, but may really be quite reserved. When the left index finger is longer than the right, you may be inclined to put on a show for everyone else. Your bluster could hide your inferiority and you may be motivated by anger rather than reason.

If both index fingers are long, you have a good ego-image and feel lovable and attractive to others. Your positive self-image bolsters your ability to deal with the world outside in an authoritative way. You display much personal power. Your upbringing has taught you to think well of your capabilities, and you are self-confident. You are able to supervise others and to achieve positions of authority. You like to be boss and are decisive and direct in your dealings with others.

Extra-long fingers are fingers that are as long as the middle finger and indicate someone who feels equal to the highest task. This extreme sense of self-confidence can deliver you to the uppermost echelon of society, providing you have the strength to back up the confidence. You exert tremendous influence over others. You are a born ruler, monarch or president. If the extra-long index fingers are accompanied by an equally strong hand, you will be dominant but not domineering.

While long index fingers indicate self-confidence, short index fingers depict an inferiority complex. You don't feel lovable (left hand) and don't think you are worthy of attention (right hand). You feel stupid and unattractive. However, it should be noted that this is how you *feel* and may not necessarily be the way you are.

Third Finger. This finger, like the index finger, is measured against the middle finger as either standard, long, short or extra long. This finger rules both emotional and mental aspects of the personality. It represents the way we use thought and feeling in our encounters to achieve our own personal ends. It also contains our love of exquisite form and beautiful emotions. Here, you express these feelings to others, particularly to those who agree with you and validate your personality. Platonic love is expressed in the third finger of the left hand, while gambling on objective outcomes or concerns is found in the right hand.

If both your third fingers are long, you are patient with your friends and finish what you start. You possess enough patience and artistic ability to top any career ladder you might choose, especially the more long-term ventures. The long third finger of the right hand indicates a willingness to gamble on the hunches represented in the left hand. A long third finger in the left hand means you are actively deciphering the instinctive dislikes of people. In general, you demonstrate a keenly developed charm that wins others over to your way of thinking and feeling. Slow to judge and criticize, you are usually well liked. Your extreme tolerance of the outer world allows you great freedom in making friends in many places. You are willing to listen when others feel like talking.

If your third fingers are extra long, you greatly enjoy gambling and speculation. "Take a chance" will be your motto, whether in scientific research or at the gaming table. You are very artistic and have the ability to express yourself in drama, art, music or poetry. Your choice of expression will be indicated by other factors in your hand, such as shape, size or structure of the fingers and hand.

If your fingers fall short of the halfway mark of the middle finger, there has been too little growth in this area of your life. Because of your impatience, you can easily trigger a negative response in others. You are the type of person who tries to speed up your friends by impatiently tapping your feet or strumming the table top with your fingers. To you, everyone is too slow, for you are the one with snap judgments and swift decisions. You are inclined to be mercenary, judging people by their outer affluence. You have a quick temper, too, but fortunately it is short-lived. You dislike detail work, like housekeeping and bookkeeping, and when it is a must, you rush through it quickly.

Fourth Finger. Surprisingly enough, your little finger packs a lot of power in a small package! Your smallest finger represents your one-to-one relationships, your intimate connections. It is also the finger of communication, for all communication is essentially one person expressing him- or herself to another. Although a speaker may talk before a large audience, he or she must reach each member individually before that communication is successful. The same one-to-one principle applies in other forms of communication, whether it is between man and woman, writer and reader or teacher and class.

Particularly, the little finger of your left hand represents your receptivity to non-verbal messages. These non-verbal communications include the unspoken emotional messages of others, as well as telepathic and psychic communications.

Long little fingers on both hands represent the ability to perceive the unseen and inaudible, making hunches reliable. If you have long little fingers, deep philosophical discussions fascinate you. You love conversations about the abstract and the unknown. You are versatile, and since your long fingers help you to pick up the "pulse" of the public, you can be a skilled businessperson in a firm where the public's needs can be met. You desire general improvement for all, including yourself.

If your little finger is very long, it will dominate all other fingers and the rest of your personality. Your greatest talent may be a combined use of body language and oratory skills that have a significant impact on others.

If your little finger is short, you withdrew your antenna to non-verbal messages early because you experienced the world as harsh. At that time, you preferred not to know what others felt. Unfortunately, this withdrawal stunted your psychic ability, and you cannot depend on your hunches. Instead, you work very hard for everything you earn in life. You arrive at conclusions rapidly and may lack caution. You must struggle, for your communication skills lack development. You generally ignore what others say and feel.

If your fourth fingers are of the standard length, you are both a competent speaker and a good listener. Aware of your environment, you have spontaneous flashes and hunches about it, but they may be infrequent. Your hunches are still more accurate than your guesses. You can stimulate growth of your ESP development by stroking your little finger. Massaging the small finger and encouraging yourself will help you to "tune in to" the abundance of information available outside the frequency of the physical senses. Train yourself to be more observant of body language and the tremors and pauses behind the voices that speak. With a little practice, you can easily rise to a higher level of communication and a broader spectrum of perception.

Combinations of Finger Lengths

As we are learning, each development, or lack of it, in the hands signifies some aspect of the personality. These developments also carry a specific significance when they are found in combination with each other. Check below to see if any of the following apply.

• If your first finger is actually longer than your second finger, you may tend to be power hungry. This is a tendency that you must guard against.

• If your first and second fingers are absolutely level with each other, your love of power is too great.

• If your first finger is much longer than your third finger, your ambition is greater than your capacity for achievement.

• If your third (ring) finger is longer than your first, you have a love of art, but no ambition to become an artist. You should support the arts, or even sustain an interest in them, to compensate for your lack of ambition.

• If both your index and ring fingers are equal, you have a great desire for fame and riches.

• When the third is longer than the second finger, you love to take risks.

• When the middle and third fingers are equal, you are also a gambler.

• If the fourth finger is almost equal to the index finger, you are diplomatic.

• If the little finger is nearly equal to the middle finger, you are extraordinarily able in the sciences.

• If your fourth finger is virtually equal to your third finger, you are versatile and can influence others. Your lively mind allows facile self-expression and fluent speech. You are an adept actor or actress with a talent for mimicry.

Warped, Stunted or Inflated Digits

Our early experiences often warp our egos and our outer selves simultaneously. Our childhood interactions with our families and friends may stunt certain developments while encouraging others to expand. In this way, our personality is shaped, and so is the physical representation of it—our hands.

So those digits that suffered malnutrition are stunted. Those that were overfed become large and important. Society is strong in its efforts to shape and control us. Its effect on us is reflected in the growth of our bones and their rigidity.

It is possible to determine the significance of each structural deviation in the hands. In general, a finger that is curved toward another indicates that the power associated with the bent finger is offered in service to the finger it bows before. Stunted fingers imply a lack of development.

If your hands are warped in ways you dislike, begin straightening them by stroking and manipulating your fingers. A steady application of stroking along with a clear mental image of the shape you desire will bring about a change.

If some of your fingers have been stunted (not allowed to grow) and you seek expansion and improvement in those areas of your life, grasp the knuckle underlying the finger you desire to change and pull gently outward, twisting and turning in a stroking motion as you stretch it. Do this while you are fully aware of your purpose. Visualizing the end result you hope to achieve, while stretching, helps reinforce your purpose.

Remember that crooked fingers can be straightened; warped fingers can be elongated and short fingers can stretch out! But the key is to change the personality trait that the deformity represents.

The following are examples of warped or curved finger growth. Do you see your hands depicted below?

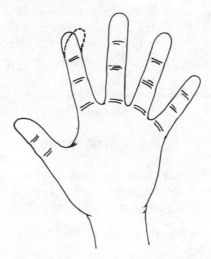

Figure 6-3. Index Finger Curved Toward Middle Finger

Figure 6-3. A curvature of the index finger toward the middle finger is quite common in our society because the environmental forces that are exerted to control a child often warp the child's self-expression in favor of behaving in accepted ways. For the most part, individualistic behavior is discouraged in the early years while parents try to "socialize" their children. The index finger here is curved toward the middle finger. This shows that the roles we play (represented by the middle finger) are more important than ourselves (first finger).

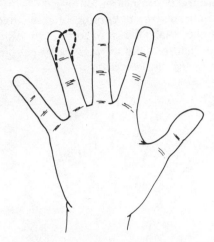

Figure 6-4. Ring Finger Curved Toward Middle Finger

Figure 6-4. The ring finger is the finger of personality—the vehicle we use to achieve personal pleasure and satisfaction through friendships and public contact. When it is curved toward the middle finger, a facade of response to societal expectations has hindered the individual's approach to others. Role-playing will dominate this person's encounters with others.

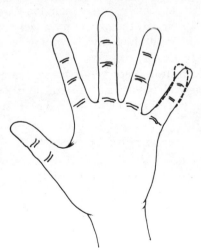

Figure 6-5. Little Finger Curved Toward Ring Finger

Figure 6-5. A little finger curved toward the ring finger is very commonly found for it represents the ability to conceal one's true feelings.

The lower the start of the warp (nearer to the palm), the more ingrained the habit of concealment is. Extreme warping of this finger reveals a person who would rather lie than tell the truth, for this is the finger of communication. The field of sales attracts many people with warped little fingers, because they excel as "con artists."

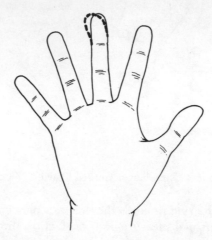

Figure 6-6. Middle Finger Curved Toward Ring Finger

Figure 6-6. A middle finger curved toward the ring finger illustrates the person who attempts to get society to give them fame. If the middle finger is curved toward the index finger, the person may seek power. In either case, this warp represents an individual who is willing to bend social roles to achieve personal satisfaction.

The next four illustrations depict four classic examples of those whose stunted fingers have been shaped and distorted by strong societal pressures, including several with combinations of warped and stunted fingers.

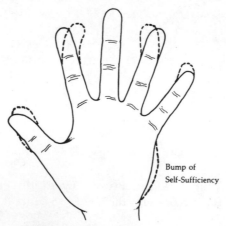

Bump of
Self-Sufficiency

Figure 6-7. The Social Animal

The Social Animal is a person whose early environment was harsh and powerful. This person bent to the will of society, thereby obeying the rules, behaving according to the dictates of others and generally doing what they were told they "should" do. Because they are unable to assert their independence, they have developed a bump of self-sufficiency. This bump of self-sufficiency indicates that they learned to meet their own needs in culturally approved ways. Their belief system and attitudes are a reflection of those who taught them because they tend to do little original thinking. They have become an amalgam of all others who influenced their training. But like weathered trees, they are hardy and have excellent survival capabilities.

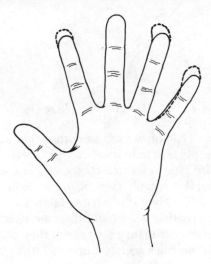

Figure 6-8. The Dissembler

The Dissembler is an individual, well aware of his or her own self-worth, who hides it under a personality that caters to other people. This person has learned to maintain the appearance of giving in to others, while maintaining a personal integrity within. They have learned the value of "white lies" and do no insist on their point of view when it would not achieve results for them. They are usually charming, yet their personal strength often pervades their amiable exterior, revealing individual power. In fact, they can become a power in the world without exercising authority or dominance.

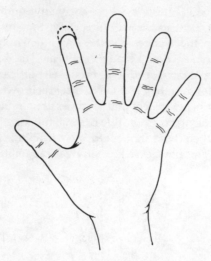

Figure 6-9. "I'm not OK, you're OK"

The most common type of stunt in growth is the "I'm not OK, you're OK" person. These people lack individuality and subordinate themselves to others. This personality type is created by societal pressure on individuals to conform. These people are easily controlled by social expectations; they are sheep who work diligently without complaint. Lacking individuality, they develop personalities that accept all others as superior to themselves. Trained to obey, to believe what they are taught, they do not question their superiors. They fulfill the roles society imposes rather than develop their own inherent powers and capabilities.

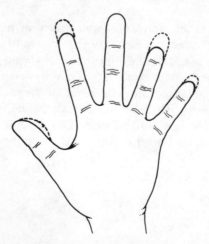

Figure 6-10. "I'm OK, you're not OK"

The "I'm OK, you're not OK" type is frequently found among people who may not respect the rights of other individuals. They feel their needs supercede those of others. While these people may be doers, people who get things done, they must guard against their need for instant gratification. Often, if given a choice, they will seek short-term rewards, just because they can realize them sooner, rather than more attractive long-term rewards.

Now that we have considered how our fingers "grow naturally" or are stunted by the forces of society, let us consider how the individual phalanges of our fingers should grow, for Mother Nature was very precise when she endowed us with her bounty. Like a leaf that tapers in gradations, the breadth of the phalanges in our fingers also narrows. We will consider the sizes of our phalanges in the next chapter.

7

Finger Phalanges

For many years, scientists have known that much information about the life of a tree can be found by examining the rings in a cross section of the trunk. Thick rings indicate a year of healthy growth in optimum conditions; whereas a thin ring means that the environment was harsh and growth was slow, nearly non-existent.

The phalanges of our fingers function similarly to the rings of a tree, providing information about growth of each phalange and its parallel aspects of the personality.

The phalanges of the fingers are the three spaces between the knuckles. The first phalange is considered to be the area from the fingertip to the "crease" of the palmar side. The second phalange is the middle area between the two creases, while the third phalange ends where the hand proper begins, the point where fingers are "cast off." As was discussed in Chapter 4, if the line where the fingers cast off is even and straight, then equal power is given to each finger. However, if the cast-off drops below a particular finger, that finger's power is considerably weakened. It is important to bear this in mind when examining the relative importance of the fingers, and their respective phalanges.

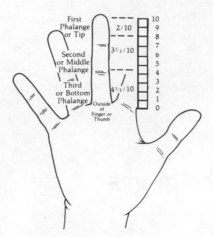

Figure 7-1. Normal Finger and Thumb Proportions

> Divide in 10 parts for measuring—tips should be 2
> parts of whole; middle should be 3½ parts; and
> the bottom should be 4½ parts.

Normally, each of the three phalanges have unequal measurement when compared to each other. If the length of the finger is divided into ten equal parts, the standard measure is that the first phalange is two parts; the second phalange will measure three and one-half parts; and the bottom phalange will measure four and one-half parts of the whole.

When examining the meanings of the individual phalanges, it is also important to consider that particular finger, because each finger is thought to represent a different area of your life. In general, your thumbs represent the strength of your will; your index fingers represent your ego and self-image; the middle fingers represent your response to societal roles and family; the third finger indicates concern in personal satisfactions, particularly with friends; and the small finger represents the area of communication, especially in close, interpersonal relationships.

For instance, if the tip of your finger is long by contrast to the standard length for the first phalange, then your personal needs become more important to fulfill. If the bottom phalange is short because the middle phalange is excessively long, then social status is far more important than physical satisfaction.

It is common to see the fourth finger with a very long-tipped phalange. These are people-oriented individuals, far more interested in psychology and philosophy than the practical world of success or physical satisfaction. They love to converse and their discussions delve into the abstract rather than physical details of daily life. It is interesting to note that these people seem to cluster together and usually find each other very compatible.

You may find variation from finger to finger, or similar measurements throughout the hand. Puffiness in a specific phalange may indicate laziness in the area of your life that the phalange represents. When the middle phalange is puffy, it denotes a lazy mind and is indicative of those who dislike study and thinking for themselves. Puffy fingertips indicate laziness about self-improvement or lack of interest in self-expression.

The famous psychologist, Abraham Maslow devised a hierarchy of human needs ranging from our basic survival requirements to the higher order of our psychological growth requirements. These needs can be further simplified and categorized into three areas; physical, social and personal needs.

Our three phalanges represent each of these three areas, beginning with the more basic lower physical needs found in the bottom phalange and ranging to the higher personal needs represented in the top phalange.

The five levels of physical needs are each represented in the bottom phalange of the four fingers and the ball of our thumbs, called the Mount of Venus. The five different areas of our social needs can be seen in the five middle phalanges. The tip of each finger relates our personal needs, which rank last in the satisfaction of our needs.

As Maslow's model of development suggests, we must first fulfill our physical requirements, then our social needs, before we can expect to pursue our personal satisfactions.

The Third Phalange

Puffiness of the third phalange may indicate laziness, selfishness and a love of physical satisfactions. If there is a "waist" or apparent inward curving when the fingers are closed, then this person likes dainty foods, clothes and surroundings. A waisted third phalange also demonstrates a delicacy of the mind and ascetic tendencies.

If your third phalange is flat, it is likely that you are a hard worker, even willing to furnish your own supplies to meet your physical needs.

If the third phalange is shorter than the standard, your interest equals only what is absolutely necessary for survival. This lack of interest in the physical arena shows that you are better suited to pursuing social skills, fulfilling social needs or improving your own self-development.

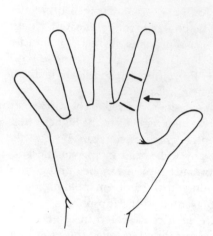

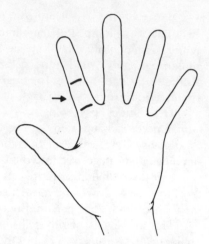

Figure 7-2A. Third Phalange of Index
Finger (left hand)

Figure 7-2B. Third Phalange of Index
Finger (right hand)

Figure 7-2B. The third phalange of the index finger on your right hand represents the objective needs of your own body for food, air, water and protection from the elements. The bottom phalange of the index finger in the opposite hand (Figure 7-2A) depicts the need for physical contact with other human beings, the need to be touched, hugged and to receive physical affection. The need to *feel* physically alive is found here.

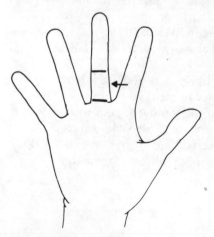

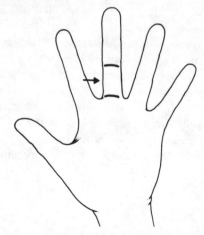

Figure 7-3A. Third Phalange of Middle
Finger (left hand)

Figure 7-3B. Third Phalange of Middle
Finger (right hand)

Figure 7-3B. The third phalange of the middle finger of your right hand represents the need for your own home and land. This is also the need to be in contact with the land, natural vegetation and animals. The same place on the opposite hand (Figure 7-3A) represents the need for our own personal space, solitude and communion with all nature.

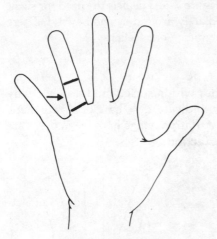

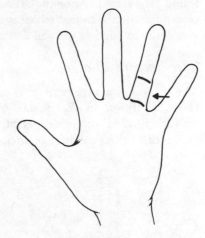

Figure 7-4A. Third Phalange of Third Finger (left hand)

Figure 7-4B. Third Phalange of Third Finger (right hand)

Figure 7-4B. The need to beautify and to appear attractive to others is found in the bottom phalange of the third finger on the right hand. Here resides the need to adorn ourselves and our homes with the luxury of beautiful things. Our drive toward external beauty can be found here. The corresponding place in the left hand (Figure 7-4A) represents the need to feel beautiful inside, to glow with happiness and good health.

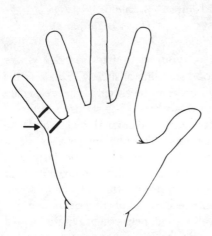

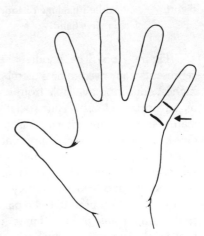

Figure 7-5A. Third Phalange of Little Finger (left hand)

Figure 7-5B. Third Phalange of Little Finger (right hand)

Figure 7-5B. The need to communicate with others and to make objective connections is found in the bottom phalange of the little finger on the right hand. This is where the need to be heard and to relate to the world around us is found. The same place on the left hand (Figure 7-5A) depicts the need for silent communication with that which is immediately around us and beyond. There is a desire to connect with all and communicate our feelings.

The Second Phalange

The second phalange represents our roles within society and how we play them. Puffiness in the phalange may indicate a lethargic or apathetic attitude toward society's expectations. A flat phalange here means you are energetic in your pursuits of social satisfactions.

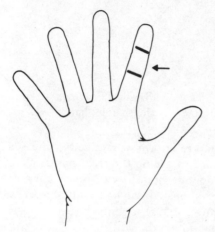 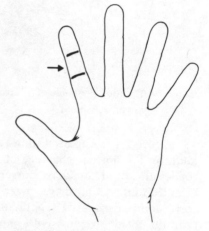

Figure 7-6A. Middle Phalange of Index   Figure 7-6B. Middle Phalange of Index
Finger (left hand)   Finger (right hand)

Figure 7-6B. The middle phalange of your right hand's index finger represents your need to be a member in good standing of society. You seek the highest education available from society in order to be accepted and respected as an upright citizen. Your social need in this phalange is status; you are a status seeker. This phalange is associated with the mental realm and the emphasis here is on social approval of your mind. This phalange is also one of practicality, so a practical mind is something for which you particularly seek recognition. In your left hand (Figure 7-6A), the same phalange represents your need to be accepted by society. You seek approval through your social connections. You need to feel a part of some recognized portion of society and find a comfortable place within it. Your feelings will help you gravitate toward that level of society in which you most naturally fit.

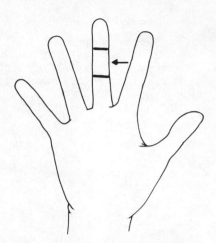

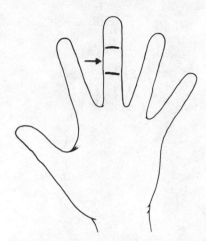

Figure 7-7A. Middle Phalange of
Middle Finger (left hand)

Figure 7-7B. Middle Phalange of
Middle Finger (right hand)

Figure 7-7B. The middle phalange of the middle finger in the right hand symbolizes society. This is where we are molded by our cultural heritage. The middle phalange of this finger demonstrates the extent to which we tend to stay within tradition, obey the law and fulfill societal expectations. Here is a representation of the tendency to adopt social roles demanded of men and women, fathers, mothers, sisters and brothers. The strength of kinship is evident here, as we can see how we mimic our role models in socially acceptable ways. Likewise, the same phalange of the left hand (Figure 7-7A) indicates whether our hearts are in the social roles we play. Indeed, it is an empty role unless we play it with feeling. This phalange will signify the tendency to find fulfilling roles, particularly fulfilling careers. This is where the "call" to a certain profession will be depicted.

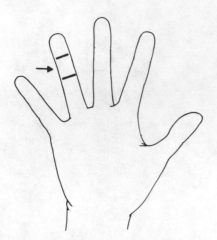

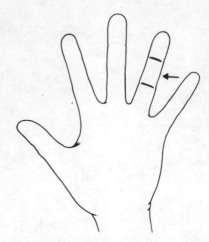

Figure 7-8A. Middle Phalange of Third
Finger (left hand)

Figure 7-8B. Middle Phalange of Third
Finger (right hand)

Figure 7-8B. When examining the middle phalange of the third finger of
the right hand, we leave social obligations, duties and needs and move into
the area of leisurely pursuits. This area of the finger is associated with the
hobbies we enjoy. If this phalange is extra long, mental skills will be your
joy. It is here that we find the extent to which we need to be entertained and
entertain others. The corresponding phalange of the left hand (Figure 7-8A)
is the place where we can see if the inner yearnings for fun are being allowed
expression. This finger has been called the happy finger and it seems to be
the area where even a demanding ego gives way to the self within and
allows it to get out and have a little fun now and then.

Puffiness in this phalange indicates an inability in social matters or the
likelihood that you will make others entertain you while you view life from
a passive position. It can indicate a love of being admired, but not wanting
to actually make the effort to earn the admiration.

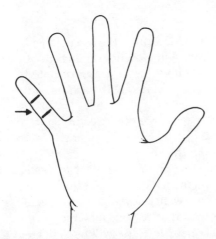

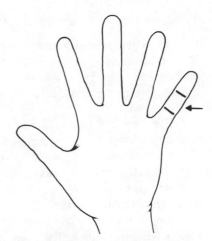

Figure 7-9A. Middle Phalange of Little
Finger (left hand)

Figure 7-9B. Middle Phalange of Little
Finger (right hand)

Figure 7-9B. The middle phalange found in the little finger of the right hand relates to your view of marriage. When it is long, it is important to you to marry within your class; however, if the phalange is short, you will not be class-conscious in your relationships. In fact, a short middle section will enable you to relate to people at every level of society, since your concerns are not limited to your own class.

If the phalange is long, it is very important that your intimates be your mental equal because mental rapport is most significant in your search for a mate. If this long middle phalange is accompanied by a short bottom phalange, your partner's physical appearance is not as important as their education, social status or the mental harmony between you.

If the middle phalange in the left hand is long (Figure 7-9A), it gives access to others' silent thoughts. If you are married to one with a similar phalange, you read each other's minds. These marriages are usually based on mental compatibility. If this phalange is short, but the bottom phalange of the little finger is long, physical appearance overrides your need for a match of the minds between you and your mate. The man with a large bottom phalange and a short middle one on the little finger admires feminine beauty and does not care if his mate is an intellectual or not. The same applies to a woman who is only looking for a handsome man. A narrow middle phalange represents a person who is not concerned with what others think, but only their own thoughts.

In some little fingers, there seem to be only two phalanges, the tip and the bottom, with virtually no middle. This denotes a person who may marry for personal reasons, but is attracted to others for physical considerations.

First Phalange of Fingertip Pads

In a later chapter, much more insight will be gained about the level of needs, seen in prints of your fingertips. That chapter will closely examine specific patterns of fingerprints and their meanings. However, it is appropriate to gain a general understanding of the meaning associated with each fingertip at this point.

The personal needs, also called "meta-needs" are discussed in depth in Abraham Maslow's book, *Self Actualization*, which is recommended to those who want to pursue this subject in depth.

Basically, once we have fulfilled both our physical and social needs, represented by the lower phalanges, we can embark on greater satisfactions of a very personal nature. Maslow identifies twenty-seven personal needs, but they are so closely related to each other that if you pursue one, the others will materialize. The needs you most need to fulfill will be indicated by your hand type, finger length and the patterns on your fingertips (covered in the chapter on Dermaglyphics).

If your fingertip phalanges are noticeably longer than average, you will work for these personal needs within this lifetime. They will be the primary movers within your personality.

These needs are present for everyone, no matter how long the fingertip phalanges are. They are simply waiting to be developed. They act like hunger, arousing the individual's motivation to meet the unsatisfying aspects of his or her lifestyle and then moving on.

Each of the fingertips represents a cluster of these meta-needs.

The tip of the index finger in the right hand represents the need for self-actualization, while the parallel tip of the opposite hand represents the need for self-realization. The left-hand index fingertip demonstrates the need to uncover the mystery of the self's identity, while the corresponding right hand tip displays the need to bring that "realization" into "actualization" or objective form.

The middle fingertip of the right hand shows the need for justice and compassion for all people—a true humanitarian need. The middle fingertip of the left hand indicates the need for divine love and acceptance of humanity.

The yearning for true beauty resides in the third fingertip of the right hand, while the need for humor that enlightens and reveals is found in the opposite fingertip. This is where the need to laugh, be happy and find humor in everything is found.

The fourth fingertip of the right hand represents the need to seek and express the truth above all else. The opposite fingertip represents the need to be united with all, to become one in the name of love. This is the seat of yearning for a higher love, a need to heal others silently through a touch or radiating thought. This is the place where the individual seeks perfect harmony to see the unseen, to know the unknowable, to feel the untouchable.

8

The Thumbs

Of the five fingers, it is the thumb, in particular, that serves to separate us from our simian predecessors. As the thumb became more flexible, we gained control over tools and weapons; and as the human brain enlarged, the scope of our ability to communicate improved.

The thumb, then, is the most important digit in the hand. Some Chinese palmists read only the thumb. Cheiro, a European palmist of the last century, believed the thumb represented the center of the brain and controlled all nervous diseases and paralysis.

Many believe that evidence of our transition from simian to human can be found in the thumb. It is in the thumb that we find the signs of authority, command, conquest, despotism and dictatorship, for it is the ruler of the hand.

Surprisingly enough, although it is not immediately apparent, the thumb is the largest digit of the hand because its three phalanges are each longer than the finger phalanges. The first and second phalanges of the thumb extend beyond the palm, while the third phalange becomes the Mount of Venus and is encircled by the life line of the hand.

As we have seen throughout this book, the concerns of the right and left brains are exhibited in the opposite hands and, of course, the opposite thumbs. Generally, your right thumb shows areas of *thought* and how they are translated into action. Many of these thoughts are the integration of what you have learned from others: parents, teachers, friends. In this way, then, they are seldom original. Conversely, your left thumb indicates certain *feelings* and their translation into action. These feelings are *always* original. These emotions arise from the inner you; they cannot be adopted from the outside.

It follows then, that the left hand represents the "primary" force—those original feelings which seek expression. The right hand is secondary, concerned with the active expression of the beliefs, attitudes and convictions that have evolved through the intellectual process.

In addition, as with the other fingers, each thumb phalange depicts certain aspects of the personality. Specifically, the tip of the thumb indicates the will. The thumb tip of the right hand represents the will of the ego, while the corresponding phalange of the left hand indicates the will of the inner, natural self. The second phalange of both thumbs relates to natural intelligence, the presence of logic in the right hand and wisdom in the left hand.

As was seen in the fingers, the third or lower phalange of the thumb represents the physical realm. In the right hand, the bottom phalange indicates the outer self, or ego, in action. It also represents the existence of physical strength, as well. The third phalange of the left hand depicts inner emotional strength, which to some extent determines outer strength.

This phalange also demonstrates vitality of feeling, health, and well-being. In addition, it represents the existence of emotional strength and stability. Again, it is evident that while cognitive or objective concerns are seen in the right hand, emotional or inner realms are represented in the left hand.

In the last chapter, we saw how relative phalange lengths demonstrated certain tendencies in each finger. The same is true of thumbs. For example, if the first phalange is short and the second long, this is a cautious person who likes to think things through before acting. However, if the tip is longer than the second phalange, then this is a risk-taker who can act fast and repent later.

In general, a sharply protruding joint under the second phalange indicates an innate sense of time and its passing. It may even manifest itself as an ability to guess the time fairly accurately. However, it is more likely that this person tends to be prompt with a sharp awareness of the passage of time. But, those who lack this protrusion also lack this inner clock. They must develop alternative ways of knowing what time it is, for they can lose track of time quite easily.

Compare your thumbs to the following illustration to determine the relative length of the phalanges of your thumbs.

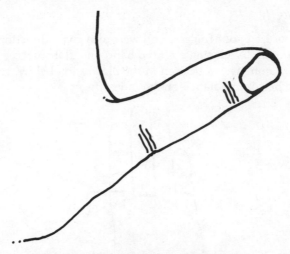

Figure 8-1. Relative Phalange Length

If the first phalange is flat, the person is calm and reasonable with an even temper. If the tip is thin and flat, cleverness and cunning are indicated.

Long thumb tips hold the ability to give orders and make decisions. This type of person has strong willpower and is very consistent. If, however, the tip is extra long in proportion to the second, there may exist a tendency toward despotism. Extra long tips in combination with an extra wide thumb show a strongly self-willed individual. As might be expected, a short thumb tip depicts an individual with a weak will who approaches life with careless indifference, or allows others to dominate.

Much can be seen about the powers of the mind in the second phalange, not only in its length, but also in the shape of the phalange. For example, if the second phalange appears to have a "waist," there exists a brilliant intellect. These people are extremely tactful, with a quick, sharp mind. They are very studious.

If the second phalange of the thumb is extra long, the person may possess a flair for using the powers of the mind. An indication of strong intuition is evident if the left hand, middle phalange is long. If the second phalange of the right hand is extended, the person is keenly able to use logic and reason. However, if the middle phalanges are longer than the tips, there may be a lack of determination and ability to carry out the ideas.

The third phalange of the thumb, otherwise known as the Mount of Venus, is very important. A much more in-depth discussion of it can be found in Chapter 12. Generally, if the mount is very large in comparison to the other two phalanges, the person is sensual, passionate, and sexually oriented. This phalange, or mount, relates to warmth, love, humanity, passion, sensuality, harmony, musical sense, and rhythm.

Thumb Length

When you measured your fingers, you were also given directions on how to measure the thumb by placing a closed hand on a flat surface. The average length of the thumb, as can be seen in the illustration below, reaches to the middle of the bottom phalange of the index finger.

Figure 8-2. Thumb Length

If the thumb reaches beyond the crease of the second and third phalange, it is considered a long thumb. People with long thumbs are tenacious, clear-minded, and determined to carry out their goals. They possess much common sense, as well as keen concentration skills. Those with long thumbs are usually intellectuals, who are generally successful in their endeavors. This is the thumb of a leader. However, if the thumb is exceptionally long, the leadership qualities become exaggerated, and these people may become domineering, interfering, ruthless, and tyrannical.

A short thumb is one that only reaches to the crease of the bottom phalange. These individuals are easily swayed by emotion and are very impressionable. They find it difficult to reach a decision or set a goal and may prefer to be submissive to the lead of someone with a long thumb. This is especially true of the person with a short thin thumb, for not only do they lack a strong will, but they possess little courage. Timidity allows these individuals to be easily influenced and quickly dominated. However, as with all other traits, this can be changed. Such a change will be reflected in the shape of the thumb.

When the emotional nature of a short thumb is combined with the pugnacity of a thick thumb, a violent nature may emerge. Again, this is something the person should work on, for it is a trait that can be controlled.

Average thumbs indicate a person who possesses both dignity and stature. These individuals would only use violence as a very last resort. These people are flexible in their ability to compromise. They can be domineering when there is a need, but they can also relax the controls if need be.

Thumb Cast-Off

Another important indicator of personality is the thumb cast-off. This can be determined by measuring the distance between the base of your index finger and the point where the thumb casts off from the hand—the point where the thumb flexes at the base.

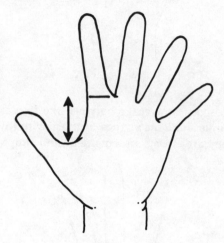

Figure 8-3. Low-Set Thumb

Figure 8-3 indicates a person who is versatile, generous and independent. This is the cast-off of an intelligent and courageous individual. These individuals are inclined to be extremists in all they undertake.

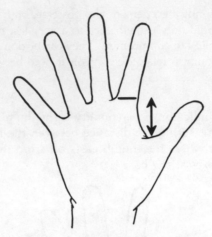

Figure 8-4. Average Cast-Off

Figure 8-4 represents an average between the two extremes of thumb positions. These people share the virtues of those with low-set thumbs, but in less measure. They are strong, independent and supportive people.

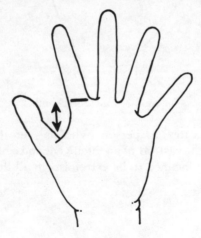

Figure 8-5. High-Set Thumb

Figure 8-5 has a short space between the base of the index finger and the cast-off of the thumb. This indicates a "closed" personality. This person may lack the ability to adapt to changing conditions.

Types of Thumbs

If the thumb is flexible and supple, extravagance is indicated. These people are generous with their time, thought, money, energy, and materials. They are sentimental, not practical.

Likewise, a firm thumb shows the opposite—a practical, cautious and secretive person. This individual is also determined, strong and disciplined.

A cramped thumb, indicated by someone who habitually holds the thumb in an introverted position, means that the person lacks self-confidence. These individuals are usually cautious and nervous.

The opposite of the cramped thumb is the bent-back thumb. This is a fairly common type, generally signifying an impulsive nature. This person may lack discipline. This tendency toward a lack of discipline can be balanced if the first phalange is relatively long.

Those with a pointed thumb tip have difficulty achieving their goals because their life energy flows out so freely. However, if a blunt thumb tip is found, the person's energy can get dammed up, and there may be a tendency toward an explosive nature. Similarly, a large first knot (the folds of skin where the finger flexes) can also dam up energy needed for achievement. Such a type denotes a lack of staying power.

A waisted thumb demonstrates an intellectual who is impulsive, diplomatic and tactful. Likewise, a thick-waisted thumb denotes a careful thinker and slow actor who is much less tactful because he or she believes their opinions are the truth and they enjoy expressing them.

As you might suspect, a person with a stiff straight thumb has a will of iron, but may be obstinate. Their reserved, slow, and cautious nature helps them to be loyal and reliable. Likewise, those with flexible thumbs do not like discord, although they are broad-minded, tolerant and adaptable. They have extravagant tastes and are generous, warm-hearted and sympathetic. They very often possess an artistic or dramatic ability.

A person who has full, wide thumbs lacks guile. These individuals are forceful, impatient, and blunt in their dealings with others.

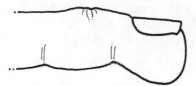

Figure 8-6. Clubbed Thumb

Figure 8-7. Flexible Thumb

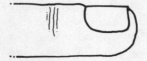

Figure 8-8. Stiff, Straight Thumb

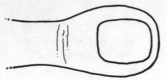

Figure 8-9. Waisted Thumb

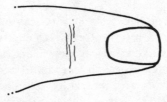

Figure 8-10. Full, Wide Thumb

Although a clubbed thumb is often genetically inherited, (see Figure 8-6), it carries certain drawbacks. It can either attract violence or the person may be vulnerable to sudden rages and loss of self-control.

Thumb Angle

Extend your thumbs away from the hands to their fullest stretch, then relax and allow them to fall to the outstretched position that is most comfortable. Match your normal position to one of the following illustrations.

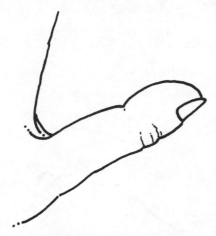

Figure 8-11. Dependent Thumb

Figure 8-11 angles upward and depicts a person who needs others in a number of ways, particularly in the area of goal achievement. A partner or group with like-minded goals can offer this willing worker the opportunity to reach mutual goals.

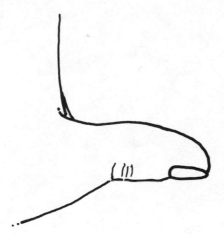

Figure 8-12. Independent Thumb

Figure 8-12 shows a right angle effortlessly formed by the resting thumb. This person can work alone and prefers individual achievements rather than the pursuit of group goals. This very independent person brooks no opposition to their ideas and actions. They have the potential for flying off in all directions. When the thumb is held widely outstretched, it displays a confident and reckless, unconventional character. However, it is stiff, so the person has the ability to control their impulses.

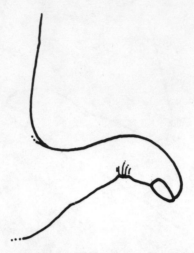

Figure 8-13. Impractical Thumb

Figure 8-13 shows someone who is always bending over backwards to please others. However, these people rarely please themselves. Their money also slides right off that sloping tip, often into the hands of the others they are trying to please.

9

The Fingernails

The fingernails can be considered the windows of the fingers. Through them, we can view the health conditions and personality traits of the individual within. By peeking through these windows, we can see what things are like in this "home" of the personality.

When given a chance, the nails grow naturally thin and transparent. But, if we become sensitive to a world we consider threatening, we close our windows by thickening and hardening our nails.

There are more nerve endings in our fingertips than anywhere else in the body. Thousands of tiny nerve endings sensitize each finger. In fact, our tips are so sensitive that we have the fingernail to protect the delicate nerve buds and fibers underneath.

Beyond the windows of the nails, we can see the intensely delicate "quick." Here, the secrets of blood circulation reveal themselves. When the nerve centers in the quick are impaired, changes will occur in the quality of the nails.

The mystery and marvel of the fingernails is considered in a passage from *Louis Lambert* by Balzac. He wrote, "When one thinks that the line separating our flesh from growing nail contains the unexplained and invisible mystery of the incessant transformation of our (vital) fluid into horn, one must admit that nothing is impossible in the marvelous transformation of the human constituting elements."

However, these mysteries do help to explain much about our behavior. And although the shape of our nails remains fixed from birth, we can use the information the shape provides to change whatever we wish about ourselves.

Perfect Nails

The "best" nails are those which match the hand type, skin texture and hand structure. For example, thick nails are "best" with thick hands, and thin nails are perfect for thin hands.

All nails should feel satiny smooth. They should be pliable, showing that the nerves are alive and elastic. The tops of the nails should be attached to the skin a moderate distance from the fingertip. The moon should be visible, indicating strong vitality and active circulation. Nails should never be bitten or chewed.

Healthy nails, or windows, also include a sturdy "sill" of cuticle. The cuticle should not be weakened with breaks or a tough edge of extra skin around the ridge. In general, cuticles should appear soft, healthy and barely noticeable.

When you hold your finger sideways, your nail should appear straight, except for almond nails, which have a gentle curve (see Figures 9-16, 9-17). If the nail is curved instead of straight, this means the person may lack energy or vitality. A healthy nail does, however, have a gentle curve from side to side. The nail color should be a rosy pink.

Fingernail Shapes

The most immediate way to unravel the "mystery" of the nails is by noting their size and shape. Your nails will be either: conical (oval), square, spatulate (triangular), oblong, round or almond-shaped. Our nails act as a pictorial representation of who we are and what we are capable of accomplishing. These "nail pictures" are definitely one of the ways our bodies communicate to us.

The most obvious picture symbolism of the nail is its size, ranging from small to medium to large. In general, large nails depict a tolerant, accepting, broad attitude. Large nails symbolize a robust person with excellent recuperative powers. The smaller the nail, the more the person works on nervous rather than physical energy. The lack of physical energy in people with small nails tends to make them more critical of others. Therefore, the larger the nail, the more broad-minded the person; the smaller the nail, the more narrow-minded.

Generally, small nails depict a high-energy metabolism, like that found in a small animal. Individuals with small nails are energetic, curious, intuitive, impulsive, quick-tempered and critical. If your nails are very small, you work almost exclusively on nervous energy.

Large nails depict the opposite extreme. They show physical strength, openness and sincerity. These people have the potential for development of mental powers and possess clear sound judgment.

However, in order to decipher the whole meaning of our nails, we must not only consider the size of the nail, but also the shape. To determine the shape of your nails, place your fingers on a piece of paper and trace the tips. Now, looking at those nails, trace the perimeter of your nails with an imaginary pen, being sure to include the line where your nail separates from the fingertip. Then recreate the imaginary nail outline, adding it to the tracing of the fingertips.

You may find that the shape of your fingernails varies somewhat from nail to nail. This is a positive sign. It means you are versatile, sharing the traits of more than one group of nail types. Check the illustrations below to see which category your fingernails match.

Oval Nails

The most common type of nails, and clearly the most practical, are oval nails. They are also called conical nails and are considered the most balanced because they appear to be a combination of the square and rounded nail types.

All the lines of this type are rounded, particularly where the nail separates from the skin at the tip. This should be nicely rounded, for if there is a straight line across, there is a physical problem present. As with all types of nails, the characteristics represented vary according to size.

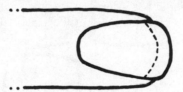

Figure 9-1. Large Fingernail

Figure 9-1 depicts a nail type associated with people who are broad-minded and idealistic. Generally, they are socially-minded and are open to companionship. These nails indicate enthusiasm for the artistic. They are extremely capable and good-natured. If the nail stretches across the width of the tip, great tolerance is shown. This individual is able to comprehend the breadth of any idea.

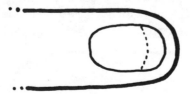

Figure 9-2. Medium Fingernail

Figure 9-2 represents a nail type belonging to people who are not quite as active or energetic as large-nail types, although they have increased their ability to be discriminating and accurate critics.

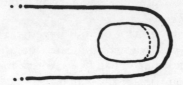

Figure 9-3. Small Fingernail

Figure 9-3 shows the nail type of a decisive person, one who is clear about what he or she thinks is positive or negative, right or wrong. This person should be careful, though, not to become dogmatic about their beliefs. Instead, he or she should be firm about their opinions, but be open to others, as well.

Square Nails

These nails are square in appearance, usually with a straight line across the bottom. In general, people with these nails stand "square" with the world. They tend to do well in systems where following orders is necessary.

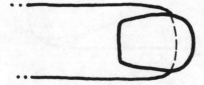

Figure 9-4. Large, Square Fingernail

The nail in Figure 9-4 nearly reaches across the entire top of the finger. These people are very careful and neat about their appearance. Their analytical ability is astounding and they are extremely discriminating. Of the square types, these are the most broad-minded, open and sincere. Their business acumen is acute and they generally enjoy material success. The bright red that generally shows through these nails indicates robust health. These nails can often be found on air-type hands (see Chapter 5).

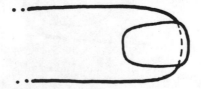

Figure 9-5. Medium, Square Fingernail

Because the nail in Figure 9-5 is smaller, people with these nails share the qualities of larger nails, but to a lesser degree. They are orderly, practical, and work hard. Noted for their common sense, they can either be discriminating or very critical. As you might expect, this hand is commonly found in the earth type.

Small nails are rarely found among this type. However, there are three other variations:

Figure 9-6: Oblong, Horizontal Fingernail

Figure 9-6 is similar to the large square nail in shape, but it lacks the height. This type of person can be aggressive in a positive way, but may be inclined toward immaturity.

Figure 9-7. Wide, Oblong, Horizontal Fingernail

Figure 9-7 indicates an inclination to look for trouble. At best, this person can be pugnacious. At worst, domineering.

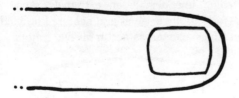

Figure 9-8. Medium, Square Fingernail with an Oval Base

Figure 9-8 indicates a person who possesses the practical common sense of the medium square nail, along with the critical sense of humor found in the conical type.

Triangular Nails

In this type, the lines of the nails generally move outward from a common point at the base. Generally, these sharp lines pictorially represent a "sharper" disposition, except in cases where the lines are "curved" and thus the personality is "softened."

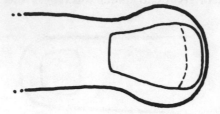

Figure 9-9. Spatulate Nail

Figure 9-9 shows the type of nail commonly found on spatulate fingers. The person possesses a critical sense of humor which, if sharpened, can be ironic. This individual is very creative and is able to find expression through art. The straight line across the bottom indicates organizational ability.

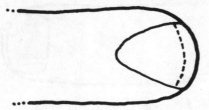

Figure 9-10. Wedge Nail

The difference between Figure 9-10 and the spatulate is the rounded bottom. This softening line depicts an extremely sensitive person. These individuals love to study by themselves and acquire knowledge. If the intellect is highly developed, their acumen as accomplished scholars is increased.

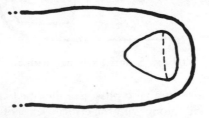

Figure 9-11A. Shell Nail

Figure 9-11A is similar to the wedge, but is much more shallow. This person has the same tendencies as those with wedge-shaped nails, but the tendencies are not as sharply developed. They often push themselves beyond the brink of their strength so they may exhibit symptoms associated with stress.

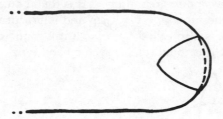

Figure 9-11B. High Shell Nail

If the shell nail (Figure 9-11B) is found high on the tip, it means the person is curious, but sometimes irritable. They enjoy a good debate on intellectual matters, but can be quarrelsome. Although quick-tempered, they show persistence in the pursuit of their own purposes. They are nervously energetic, and sometimes restless.

Narrow Vertical Nails

In general, these nails are long and narrow and indicate people who lack versatility because they are singular and straight in their pursuits. This is a picture of someone who has "narrow" interests rather than the broad-minded outlook of those with larger nails.

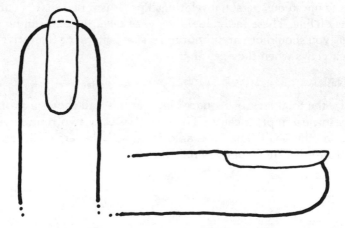

Figure 9-12. Oblong, Vertical Nail

Figure 9-12 has a long narrow nail with a straight top and a slightly rounded bottom imbedded in the flesh on either side. This person has a good disposition and is easy to get along with. These individuals are robust, but inclined to be timid. It is their lack of courage that keeps them from being assertive. This nail is never red and instead often appears to be blue at the base. This shows poor circulation. If it is found on a pointed fingertip, there is an inclination toward mysticism and impracticability.

This nail type is also called *sensitive* if it is found on a sensitive hand type, or *psychic* if it is found on a psychic hand type.

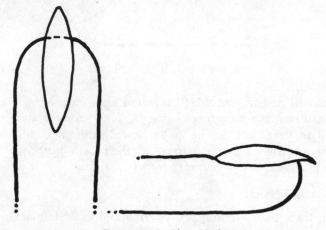

Figure 9-13. Claw Nail

Figure 9-13 is a long thick nail that is curved as well as narrow. This indicates tempestuous personal relationships. It is a nail that is considered excessively feline. These individuals are very talkative and can be vicious. However, you should be careful not to receive a literal or figurative scratch from their claws when they get angry.

Round Nails

Generally, the total lack of "square" lines in this nail shows a pronounced tendency toward impracticality. There are basically two round nail types: the large and the small. The traits associated with the large nails are clearly diminished in the small rounded nails.

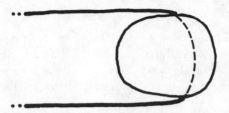

Figure 9-14. Filbert Nail

The large circle of a nail covers nearly the whole fingertip in Figure 9-14. This circular nail lacks the practicality of the square nail and is inclined to possess a dreamy nature filled with visions. These people often present their ideas to others as a gift. Their forte is not accomplishment as much as broad vision. Although they are unrealistic, they are very broad-minded, tolerant and exceptionally easy-going. In general, they possess a strong constitution and much physical stamina.

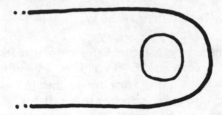

The type of nail in Figure 9-15A represents restricted development because of lack of physical stamina and diminished energy. Those with this nail type should be careful to use their energy wisely and take care of themselves physically. The nearer the nail is to the top (Figure 9-15B), the more quarrelsome they can be. However, a nutritious diet and plenty of rest can offset this tendency.

Figure 9-15B. High Corn Kernel Nail

Almond Nails

These nails look like an almond nut. They are unique, since they are the only nails that are naturally rounded from base to tip. The gentle, soft curves of this nail indicate a sensitive emotional nature. The people who have these nails are gentle and courageous. They have lucid perceptions and a love of beauty.

There are two of these almond types; the water type with a rounded bottom much like teardrop, and the fire type with narrow base that looks like a flame.

Figure 9-16. Almond Water-Type Nail

People with this nail type (Figure 9-16) are placid and easy-going. They tend to flow with the currents. However, they are not robust or energetic, but rather retiring and even shy. They are inclined to impracticality and are very sensitive. They are often absorbed in mysticism or religion. A strong aesthetic feeling gives them discrimination and their taste is conservative and refined. These exceptional types have an excellent imagination; however, they can become egotistical and selfish.

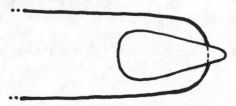

Figure 9-17. Almond Fire-Type Nail

Great courage, clarity of perception and a vivid imagination are represented in the nail in Figure 9-17. Great love of beauty and an aptitude for emotional expression are found here. These nails are generally thicker than the water type and seem to be naturally polished. A happy, healthy disposition is indicated, although a potential for egotism and selfishness is also present. This person is usually quite generous and demonstrative.

Curved or Flat Nails

Nails normally grow with a curvature from side to side, with a gentle slope extending the length of the nail. If we assume then that our bodies are naturally inclined to be healthy, ten nails that grow "unnaturally" mean there is an indication of some type of physical impairment.

A decidedly humped nail warns of serious lung problems while nails that are humped only in the middle indicate bronchial problems or a tendency to catch colds. Slight humping can occur in women during their menstrual period, especially if they are robust to start with. High-strung, nervous females also show this slight phenomenon, and it can indicate a need for a gynecological check-up.

Flat nails indicate nervous exhaustion. It is as if the nail collapses because it lacks enough energy to maintain its normal position. When the condition is severe, the nails become concave and the tip begins to grow, curling upward. This is a result of extreme mental effort which drains vitality. This is a common phenomenon, during final exam time in colleges, especially for people with shell-shaped nails.

Thick and Thin Nails

The thickness of the skin should match the texture of the nails. Therefore, thick nails should accompany thick skin. Likewise, if the skin is nearly transparent, the nails should be the same.

Thick-skinned people with thick nails are not easily hurt by others for they have tough hide between them and the world. It is easy to see then how thin-skinned, thin-nailed people are sensitive to the world. People with little protective covering are easily hurt.

Nail Texture

The texture of the nail also should match the skin. Silky satin skin should have similarly smooth nails, while rough skin should have dull nails. This is because rough skin is generally thick and nails that are thick appear dull.

The thin, shiny, smooth nails are those of sensitive people with great discrimination and a fine aesthetic sense. Those with thick dull nails lack that same aesthetic appreciation.

Hard, Soft, Brittle, or Flexible Nails

The texture of your nails can be used to describe the evolution of your attitude toward the world. Small children normally have flexible nails, reflecting an attitudinal resiliency. Their nerves are alive, making the nail pliable, a nail that easily bends without breaking. This is the natural state of your nails and your being. However, our response to the difficulties of life is assimilated in the nails and they often become hard and thick. As might be expected, hard and thick nails show a lack of sensitivity.

Likewise, soft nails represent a person who is easily conditioned, impressed and influenced by the world around them. This person can easily be considered a "soft touch." If the nails are extremely soft, the person probably lacks will power.

Brittle nails depict a "brittle" person who is rigid, but lacks the strength to carry out his or her convictions. This person can be easily broken under stress. Fixed opinions have left this person resistant to change. Thick brittle nails will withstand more stress than thin brittle nails. These individuals have thick exteriors and very fixed ideas about life.

In their most natural state, nails are flexible, with the power to bend, but not break in the storms and tempests of life. If your nails are thin and flexible, you dare to experience anything. If they have thickened, you have become more cautious.

Nail Color

Like the complexion of the exterior skin, the fingers beyond the window of the nail can tell us about the individual state of health.

Pink nails show an outgoing temperament and good health. These nails will turn white when pinched, but will return to pink when the pressure is alleviated. If, however, the return of color is slow, low blood pressure is indicated.

Red nails indicate a violent temper. This is a person who is prone to high blood pressure and possible heart problems. Conversely, white nails lack the intensity of red nails. This person lacks red corpuscles. The condition is associated with anemia. In general, physical energy is lacking because of poor circulation and low blood flow. This could be expressed in the personality as coldness to others. Nails that are white in the middle but pink at the outer edges are likely to be an indication of a person who has short fits of rage; however, these are rarely malicious.

If you find any tinge of blue, there is a probability that the heart is not functioning normally. At first, you will notice that the base of the nail is blue, then the coloring creeps upward. During a coronary, the nails are so dark blue that they may appear almost black. As the attack passes, oxygen floods the blood stream and the darkness vanishes.

Dark tips on your fingernails are a sign of kidney failure. Scientists at the University of Mississippi Medical Center have found that a half-dark nail is a "highly specific sign" of this disorder.

Have you ever wondered why white spots appear on your nails? These are also called liver spots and indicate a temporary liver disorder due to emotional conflict or dissappointment. This occurs with regular frequency in people who are very sensitive and emotionally susceptible. The spots act as a warning to take care of any liver dysfunction. There always is an accompanying loss of vitality. You can estimate the time of this emotional incident by considering that it takes six months for the nail to grow outward from the cuticle.

Black spots usually indicate sorrow or grief.

The area of your life that has been affected can be determined by using the following chart to find the meaning of the spots on your nails.

	White	Black
First Finger	gain and profit	loss and sorrow
Second Finger	journey	loss of reputation, dignity
Third Finger	honor, wealth	foreshadowing of a sad event
Fourth Finger	success in commerce	business failure

White spots growing together, taking over the nail surface and thereby obscuring the clarity and transparency of the nail, are a sign of hypersensitivity, which could result in severe liver disorders.

The Nail Cuticle and Moon

Many people consider the cuticle to be the annoying part of the nail that splits or frays, but the cuticle is actually an organ of touch. It is a medium of external impressions to the nerves. There are minute spiral ridges of cuticle, and these ridges correspond to depressions on the inner surface. These provide lodging for the soft pulpy skin called "papillae."

An elastic cuticle is a healthy cuticle. However, not everyone has retained the vitality of this area since many cuticles become withered, frayed, split, ridged or spread out.

If your cuticle has spread and is grown over the nail, as if to cover it completely, you are most likely trying to hide your sensitivity, to cover the perceptions and feeling represented in the moon. If the growing cuticle is also tough, it means you want to present a tough "facade" and probably will.

Frayed or split cuticles show cuts to your vanity, painful incidents that "cut you to the quick." All cuticles in this condition need soft cream to soothe them, as well as soft touches of affection to heal the wounds the self has endured.

If you have a ridged cuticle that is smooth and rounded, but rises in an uneven ridge around the nail, you have built up efficient defense mechanisms and are able to take a lot of the "tough stuff" that is dished out.

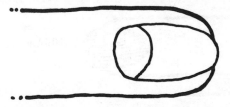

Figure 9-18. Moon on Fingernail

The moon on your fingernail represents feeling and perception. If the moon cannot be seen, it is because the cuticle has grown to cover it. If this condition exists, it means you must work harder to increase your degree of perception and sensitivity.

Like the moon of the solar system, the moon of your nails represents feelings. The actual moon on the nail is a full circle—or a full moon. The further back the cuticle is, the more potential there is for feeling and perception.

In some people, the moon is completely hidden and thereby totally submerged in the unconscious mind. The longer the nails, the further the reach of the unconscious mind. For example, a high moon on a short nail represents a more shallow, but conscious mind. A narrow nail represents a deep unconscious, but it is relatively small. A short, wide nail represents a very large subconscious, but it is shallow. A very small nail represents both a shallow and narrow subconscious.

In addition, large moons show a strong heart, good circulation and generally fortunate circumstances. This type of moon is usually found on each nail, or on none at all.

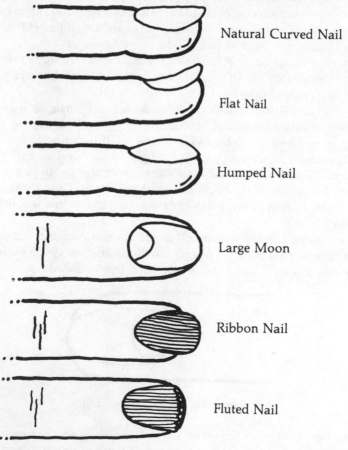

Figure 9-19. Nail Types

Nail Disorders

When the nails are even and smooth, the filaments that form them are all of one size. In their natural state, the appearance of the nails is uniform and smooth. Any abnormality in the nail indicates some type of problem.

When different filaments are being grown, ridging appears. This may represent a disorder in the nervous system. If the nail is white or bluish, it indicates a delicacy in the lungs caused by poor circulation.

When fluted, any existing condition is becoming more severe. If the nails are brittle and growing away from the quick, the case is serious. Shell-shaped nails are very susceptible to ridging and fluting. These grooves originate under the cuticle and grow out with the nail, taking four to six months to leave the end. The groove is caused by a trauma, and the effects of the trauma recede in the time that it takes for the groove to leave the nail end. You can estimate when the trauma occurred by the placement of the groove. If there is a line in each fingernail on a hand, that whole side of the nature was affected. If the grooves appear on both hands, the total person was affected.

Nail Miscellany

• Nail polish is detrimental to perfect health and function of the nails. Artificial fingernails can damage the nails badly and result in health problems. They shut off circulation, as does nail polish. Interestingly, artificial nails are manufactured in the form of the nail type which tends toward bronchial or tubercular problems.

• After a violent temper tantrum, the nails become softer and remain so for some time.

• If all your nails are smooth, but one is ridged, a strong interest and aptitude for whatever the finger stands for is indicated.

• People often bite their nails without being conscious of what they are doing. This behavior has its roots in nervousness. They are turning unexpressed hostility toward others onto themselves. If this behavior is continued for a long time, the tip of the finger itself becomes bulbous and the sensitivity of touch is lost. The end of the finger becomes very thick, forming a bulb or pad around which the nail will grow.

• If the natural nail tip is bulbous and large, the nail seems to grow in a curve around the tip, as if it were attempting to cover it.

10

Primary Palm Imprints

It is important to consider the lines crossing the palms of your hands as *imprints* of your energy level and potential. The three major lines—the heart, head, and life lines—are like rivers that separate the palm into three fields. Generally, the more lines the person has on their palms, the more energy there is flowing through the three fields. If the imprints of your lines are varied and intricate, they indicate a life of varied and intricate experiences. If the lines are tortured, frayed, angular, and chaotic, you are apt to be uptight, confused and complex. And so, just as we used the nails to look into the fingers, we can look into the rivers of palmar lines and see the image of our life reflected there.

Generally, the hypersensitive person has instantaneous reactions to every event that touches him or her. There is no lag between experience and expression. There is an event and then a response through the nervous system. This pattern of physiological responses creates many, many fine lines in the palm, which represents the conduit through which electro-magnetic energy passes. So, you are apt to find hundreds of tiny lines on the hands of those who are extremely sensitive. But, these people, in particular, are most vulnerable to a breakdown of the nervous system, since that multitude of lines can also short-circuit the energy that flows through them.

The opposite extreme is the hand with only the three basic, essential lines—the heart, head and life lines. Lacking the fine lines to pick up any undercurrent through which the more subtle aspects of human experience might be perceived, this person has only the most basic responses to experiences. In addition, this reflects a slower ability to react to situations.

But, it is not only necessary to consider the amount of lines, but also the depth of them. A picture of the person's speed in sensory perception is seen in both the quality, and the number of lines. If the lines are fine and numerous, the person's sensory perception is accelerated. Electrical impulses are transmitted from the sense organs to the nerve centers with speed. As the senses see, hear, smell, taste, and touch, an electrical process occurs that quickly translates the experience into a visualization, thus stimulating a reaction. Thicker and deeper lines mean that sensory perception is slower, more primitive and instinctive. The fewer the deep lines, the more primitive the person.

It is important to remember, though, that we are not only a sum of the physiological events associated with sensory perception. In our development, we have groomed a conscience, which also inhibits or otherwise directs our responses. Therefore, the speed of our reactions to an event is based on the speed of our perceptions, but also regulated by our inhibitions or lack of them.

When the main head, heart and life lines are all long and clearly marked, a strong character and the ability to make the most of opportunities are indicated. Clearly marked lines lack the confusion associated with lines that are not as apparent.

Nowhere is our individuality more evident than in the lines of our hands. Since we become accustomed to the palmar lines of our own hands, it is easy to assume that other people's hands must look like ours. This couldn't be further from the truth. The reality is that our hands, and particularly our palmar lines, express our individual uniqueness.

Just for fun, the next time you are in a room with a group of friends, relatives or even co-workers, take a look at their hands. You will be amazed at the differences—even among close relatives!

Life, Head and Heart Lines

Before we learn about the vast differences between hands, let us first examine the three major lines. These lines develop during the embryonic period and are evident by the fifth month of prenatal growth. Each line appears as part of a particular phase and aspect of embryonic growth.

The life line, which curves from just below the index finger, encircling the thumb toward the wrist, is developed as the nervous system grows, and so represents the nervous system and the individual's vitality.

The head line, which also begins below the index finger and stretches across the hand, ending below the third or fourth finger, develops in sequence with the digestive system. This line also represents mental activity.

Unlike the other two lines, the heart line begins on the opposite side of the hand and then ends under the first or second finger. The heart line, as its name suggests, develops along with the cardiovascular system. It represents the environment's effect on the individual.

As we have discussed earlier, the right and left hands reflect two opposite realms—the intuitive and the cognitive. It is important to remember, then, that the lines of the left and right hands are also associated with these two realms.

For example, the life line is the river of response to the world as it *feels* to the individual. The life line in each hand shows that we feel in two different ways. The life line of the right hand represents how we feel physical sensations, as in "I feel healthy, energized, weak, sick, exhausted, pain or pleasure." It is the representation of *objective* feelings. Likewise, the life line of the left hand represents *subjective* feelings, as in "I feel happy, sad, fulfilled, deprived, good about myself, or insecure."

The head line, in general, is concerned with our intelligence and our intellect, but in the right hand, it is indicative of how we think rationally and logically. It portrays our ability to perceive the world using objective information and formulating logical thoughts. But, the head line of the left hand illustrates our ability to use a more intuitive thought process. Here, we see how capable we are of solving a problem just by "knowing" the answer, without using logical thought. The capacity for gleaning the entirety of a situation intuitively, rather than analyzing and breaking it down to a logical sequence, is found in the head line of the left hand.

Both the head and life line originate on the radial side of the palm (closest to the thumb). This means that both these lines are concerned with the *personal* experience of the individual represented in the ulna side. As we have seen, the head line is concerned with thought, while the life line is associated with feelings; however, both these processes are internal—they are contained wholly within the individual.

The third major line of the heart is quite different in that it is concerned with the interplay between the individual and the environment. This line begins on the ulna side of the palm and is thus able to carry messages from the outside in. The ulna side of the palm (little finger side) represents the entrance door for input from the outside world.

The heart lines of both hands are the rivers to the heart—the stream of thoughts, feelings and experience that pulses through each of us and shapes who we become. The heart line reflects our dependence on the environment to nurture us. The heart line of our right hand shows our need for physical recognition, such as smiles of approval, hugs of affirmation or words of approbation. The negative or positive opinions of others, which are objectively expressed, flow along the right-hand heart line to help shape the self-image that is represented in the index finger. Likewise, the heart line of the left hand shows the need for emotional reassurance—to feel the silent messages of love and acceptance from others. Again, these silent messages that originate from others are transported along the currents of the heart line in the left hand to the index finger. An example of this kind of force that shapes us, is the teacher who may verbally approve of us, but we "pick up" his or her true dislike of us. That message, too, travels along the heart line to shape our self-image, represented in the index finger.

The Seven Major Lines

The seven major lines are composed of the three most essential lines and the second group of major lines. The three most basic lines will be found in every hand and were described above. Of the second group of major lines not all are found in every hand, but if they are present, their message is important. They speak of the satisfaction the individual is gaining from his or her life, and in what areas satisfaction is most likely to reward effort.

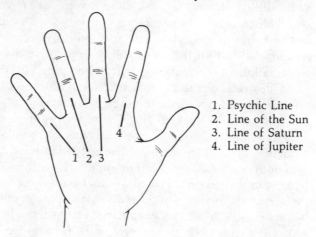

1. Psychic Line
2. Line of the Sun
3. Line of Saturn
4. Line of Jupiter

Figure 10-1. Major Secondary Lines

The line of Jupiter is rare, but denotes personal fame and satisfaction and individual success in high places, particularly as a leader or authority figure.

The line of Saturn shows a reward for work, particularly in careers which are approved of by society. It indicates satisfaction with material success and status.

The line of the Sun (also called **the line of Apollo** or Uranus) denotes personal satisfaction by utilizing talents in a vocation or avocation. It is called the line of happiness by some, the line of brilliance by others and is often interpreted as bringing money and success through talented expression.

The line of Mercury, or **the psychic line,** shows interpersonal relationships and their satisfaction or dissatisfaction. Because it shows both of these, it is sometimes not a favorable line. If it is lacking, the person may be out of touch with the rest of society. This person will not react when prodded. Instead he or she will remain aloof and unaffected.

The psychic line is also called the line of Hepatica, the line of the liver or the line of sympathy. It is a health line that indicates the physical result of interpersonal relationships. If the line is straight, long and deep, it shows a person who has direct, clear and deep relationships with others. This person is not only emotionally healthy, but has a healthy psyche and body. If the sympathetic responses to others are chaotic, fragmented, conflicting or otherwise confusing, this will be reflected in this line. The most direct physical effect of a damaging emotional relationship is on the liver—hence the name, liver line.

Because palmistry, or the study of the major lines, is the most ancient area of hand analysis, we will review it in depth. In this chapter, we will consider many examples of the individual variations of the three major lines and their meanings. The next chapter will examine the second group of major lines and the other lines, which influence behavior and personality, called minor lines and influence lines.

But in general, we can consider the following tendencies in all palmar lines:

• Any lines that curve upward suggest ambition, action, upward or outward movement. For example, lines of the second major group, which begin at the bottom of the hand and travel upward toward the fingers of Jupiter, Saturn, Apollo and Mercury, manifest activity and striving for success.

• Little lines that droop downward indicate disappointment and relaxed ambition. Also, if any of the lines are broken, qualities associated with that line have been weakened. A solid line is a stronger line.

• Remember, the three phalanges are related to physical, social and personal needs of the individual. Tiny "worry lines" on the physical phalange indicate worry over health and property. If worry lines are apparent on the social phalanges, there is anxiety over status, position and intelligence. Finally, if these lines are seen in the uppermost personal phalange, it is evidence of concern over spirituality and worthiness.

• Shallow lines restrict the energy flow and indicate less activity. Conversely, deep lines allow the passage of much energy and indicate intense activity.

But after looking at general rules for the lines, we need to consider the various permutations for the major lines.

Life Line

We look to the life line, which encloses the Mount of Venus, as an indication of the strength of the constitution, physical vitality, capacity for living and the ability to enjoy it. In general, if the life line encircles the Mount of Venus in varying degrees of depth, it represents the variations of physical vitality. If it is full and high, the person has the greatest capacity for a full, wide life, particularly as it pertains to physical activity.

The life line in each hand represents different realms. We can see our inherited physical and emotional stamina, as well as strength, in our left hands. In the life line of the right hand lies the clue to our current state of health and vitality, as well as physical strength.

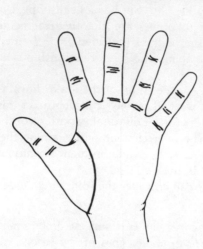

Figure 10-2. High Life Line

A high life line (Figure 10-2) starts on or very near the mount of Jupiter and indicates a highly ambitious person.

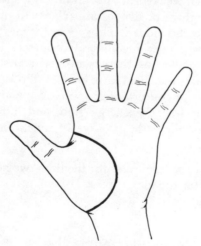

Figure 10-3. Broad Life Line

Figure 10-3 depicts a person who has plenty of vitality, a sound and healthy constitution and who will probably live to a ripe old age. An expansive person, a passionate lover. This person is devoted in their home life and also possesses stamina and endurance. If this life line surrounds a high Mount of Venus, it indicates a person of action. If the mount is flat, the person is physically vigorous.

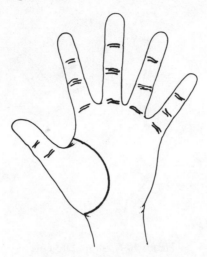

Figure 10-4. Small Life Line

A small life line (Figure 10-4) will curtail the extent of activities the person is involved with, and instead indicates a preference for small projects. This person possesses vitality, although it is more limited, as is their lifestyle. This person prefers mental activities to physical, and, therefore, tends to be a more emotional lover.

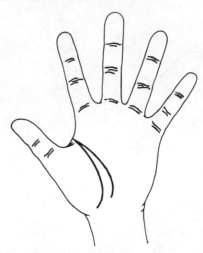

Figure 10-5. Double Life Line

Figure 10-5 appears when a person has very strong feelings and sensations. This is a very passionate person, since his or her life line is reinforced.

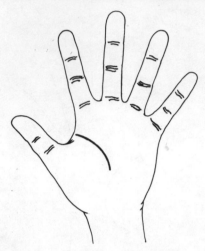

Figure 10-6. Short Life Line

If a short life line (Figure 10-6) is found in both hands with no other support lines, a lack of vitality and instinctive survival skills may be indicated.

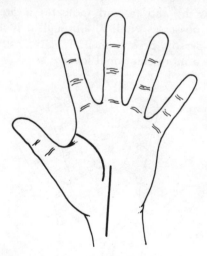

Figure 10-7. Life Line with Support

If there is a support line close enough to a short life line, then a bridge exists which can draw energy from the support line to alleviate any lack of energy in the short line. As depicted in Figure 10-7, the fate line is assisting a short life line. This line formation also indicates a change in one's lifestyle.

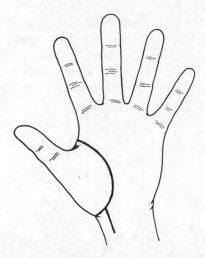

Figure 10-8. Life Line with Travel Line

In hard hands, the travel line shows a desire for change, while in soft hands, it indicates a tendency toward escapism. A life line with a strong "home-body" curve (line curves around the thumb) and an equally strong travel line (Figure 10-8), depicts a person who is torn between their desire to stay home and the longing to get away. However, their strong "home" feelings mean they will always establish a "home" for themselves and that they will always have ties to their original home area.

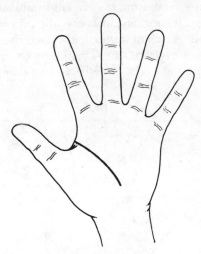

Figure 10-9. Straight Life Line

A life line that does not curve around the thumb but moves out into the hand (Figure 10-9) shows a person who is restless at home. This person will travel, probably leaving the home territory for good. This person may never settle anywhere, since little satisfaction is found in being devoted to home.

If the travel line is long and deep, the person is likely to travel to faraway places. It may also manifest in a love of books about exotic places. Travel lines in the right hand show a desire for earthly adventure.

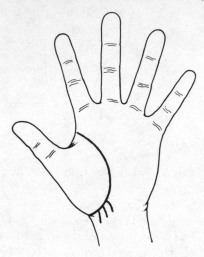

Figure 10-10. Small Travel Lines

A life line with small lines off of it (Figure 10-10) shows a person who will often enjoy getting away from the life environment, but will always be drawn to return home. If short and shallow, the person is inclined to small trips of short duration. A lack of travel lines means the person is completely satisfied with the home environment. This home environment can refer to an entire region, indicating a lack of desire to travel beyond its boundaries.

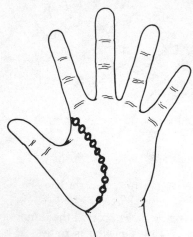

Figure 10-11. Chained Life Line

Figure 10-11. A chained life line indicates a weaker constitution because the energy is not flowing smoothly. There is also a tendency to try to do two activities at the same time, but neither receives the benefit of full attention.

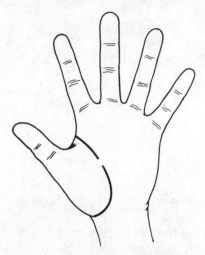

Figure 10-12. Broken Life Line

Figure 10-12. A break in the life line shows a breakdown of energy for which remedial tactics are needed to bridge the gap. Rest, nourishment, and relaxation are all positive mending processes.

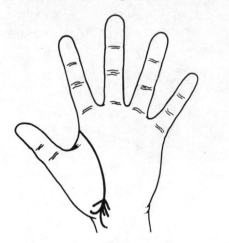
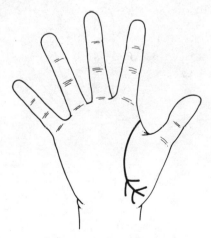

Figure 10-13. Tasseled Life Line   Figure 10-14. Tasseled Life Line

A tasseled ending to the life line (Figures 10-13 and 10-14) indicates a person who ends each cycle with depleted energy and probably frayed nerves. For them, each cycle of activity may end in exhaustion.

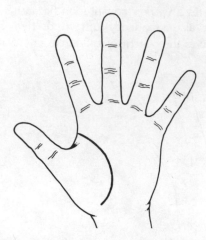 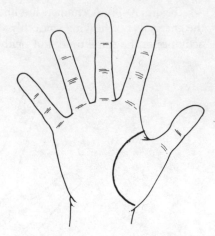

Figure 10-15. Fire Life Line　　　　Figure 10-16. Earth Life Line

When the left-hand life line curves to the base of the thumb (Figure 10-15) the person is emotionally alive and able to feel extremes. This person continually feels a full range of emotions.

When the right-hand life line curves to the base of the thumb (Figure 10-16), the person feels extremes in the physical sense. He or she is very sensitive to physical sensations—heat of the skin; pain or pleasure of the body; or even the movement and stretching of muscles.

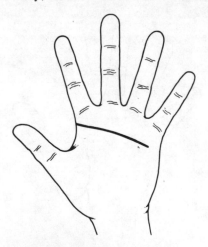 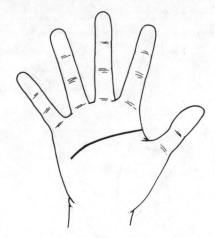

Figure 10-17. Water Life Line　　　　Figure 10-18. Air Life Line

A centered life line on the left hand (Figure 10-17) indicates strong intuitive skills. A person with this line can "know" without reasoning.

A centered life line on the right hand (Figure 10-18) indicates a person with remarkable mental faculties. Their strength lies in their ability to be logical—building concepts logically, or breaking down an idea and analyzing it. It is the line of an intellectual who yearns for knowledge.

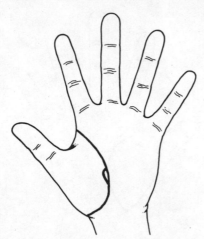

Figure 10-19. Island on Life Line

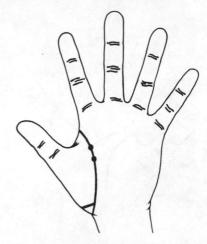

Figure 10-20. Black Dots on the Life Line

An island on the life line (Figure 10-19) shows a pattern of division of energy. This figuration reflects certain influences on health and a tendency toward nervousness.

Black dots on the life line (Figure 10-20) show physical problems due to a "jolt" to the nervous system, either actual or emotional. If red, a high fever is probably indicated. A dark spot can also relate to an accident or wound.

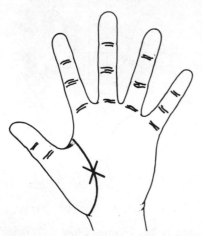

Figure 10-21. Cross on the Life Line

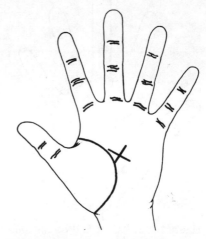

Figure 10-22. Cross Outside Life Line

A cross anywhere on the line (Figure 10-21) indicates an incident that may be difficult to handle, or a potentially stressful situation or obstacle.

A cross outside the line (Figure 10-22) usually means a change of location for the person.

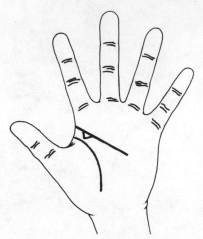

Figure 10-23. Double Life Line with Pyramid

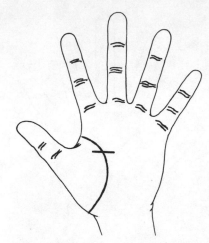

Figure 10-24. Line Crossing Life Line

An inverted pyramid on a line above the life line (Figure 10-23) shows that the individual received an uplifting start in life through positive relations with parents or guardians at an early age.

A line crossing very high on the life line (Figure 10-24) at this angle shows a concern about an obstacle or barrier that needs to be overcome.

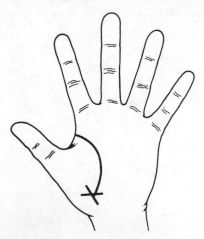

Figure 10-25. "X" at End of Life Line

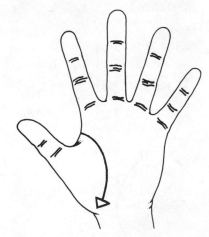

Figure 10-26. Triangle Close to Wrist

A cross at the bottom of the life line (Figure 10-25) shows a happy old age!

A triangle close to the wrist (Figure 10-26) indicates a person with diplomacy and tact.

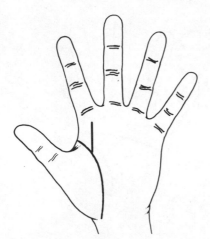

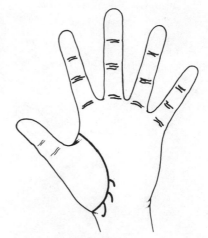

Figure 10-27. Line Rising from Life Line

Figure 10-28. Drooping Lines on Life Line

A line shooting off near the tip of the life line is a most fortuitous sign. A line rising from the life line (Figure 10-27) denotes success through ability, pluck and determination.

The drooping lines in Figure 10-28 show a possibility of financial loss or illness. This person tends to expend energy, sometimes with little or no gain.

Head Line

This is the line of the intellect. In general, the deeper and clearer the head line is, the deeper you delve into that area of the mind and the clearer your comprehension. In the right hand, a long head line shows intellectual power while the same formation in the left hand depicts intuitive awareness.

Generally, a short head line in the right hand indicates a limited interest in intellectual subjects. A short line in the left hand indicates a lack of receptivity to ideas, and particularly, inspiration. Because of this, any intuitive powers that are possessed, may lay dormant or at least will be underdeveloped.

The length of the head line indicates how much persistence the person has. (Combine with the thumb tip reading for accuracy.) The length shows the scope of perception.

If the line is very straight, the person works best mentally with facts and logic. If the line slopes, forming a curve, there is the presence of imagination. The greater the curve, the grander the imagination.

If the line is wide and thick, it may show a pituitary gland deficiency which interferes with decision-making and clarity. This person laughs and cries easily.

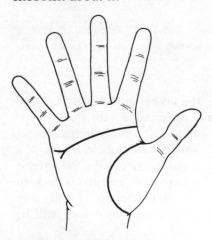

Figure 10-29. Businesslike Head Line

Figure 10-30. Intellectual Head Line

A horizontal head line (Figure 10-29) shows a strong business acumen.

The formation in Figure 10-30 shows an intellectual, who may be snobbish about it.

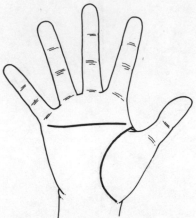

Figure 10-31. Forked Head Line

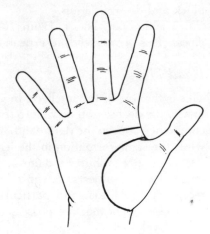

Figure 10-32. Short Head Line

A fork at the end of the head line (Figure 10-31) is the configuration of a person who is versatile. This is a common head line formation.

Figure 10-32 shows a line close to the life line and represents a timid nature. The person lacks a strong adventurous spirit. He or she may be inclined toward materialism, too.

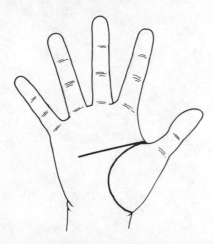

Figure 10-33. Combined Life and Head
Lines

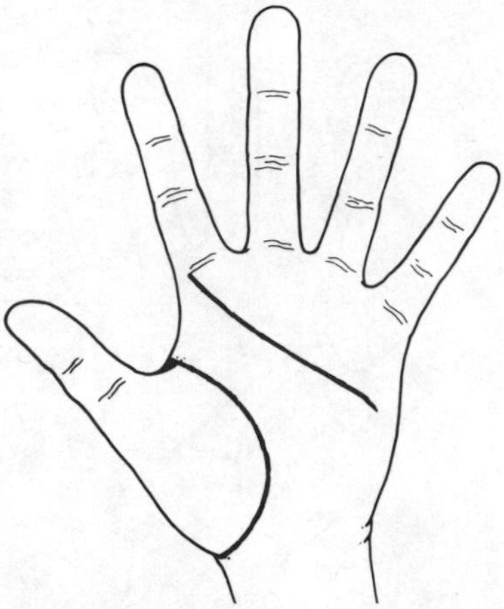

Figure 10-34. Head Line to Index Finger

When the life and head lines run together (Figure 10-33), it reflects an extremely cautious person. This person is sensitive to criticism and can be quarrelsome if placed on the defensive.

An uplifting sign! When the head line points to the index finger (Figure 10-34), it shows a sign of brilliance.

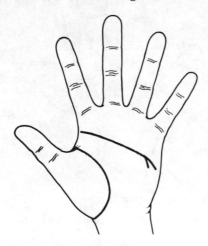

Figure 10-35. Head Line with Long
Fork

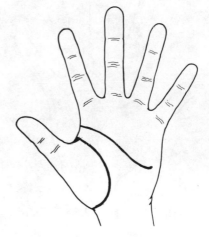

Figure 10-36. Curved Head Line

A long fork (Figure 10-35) shows an enterprising personality. This person is inventive and resourceful.

Figure 10-36 shows a person with an aptitude for success and the ability to make money. Whenever the head line curves up, earning ability is indicated.

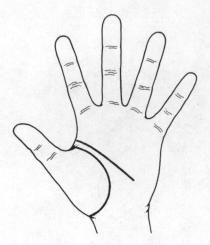

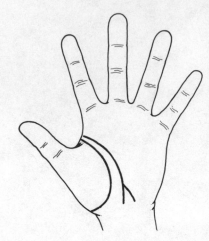

Figure 10-37. Imaginative Head Line

Figure 10-38. Curved Head Line with Fork

A head line that curves down (Figure 10-37) represents an active imagination. It also depicts an artistic nature.

The split line in Figure 10-38 denotes a person with divided goals.

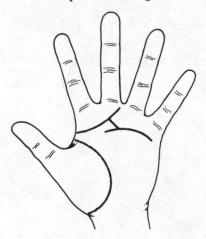

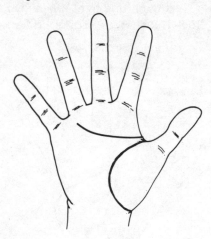

Figure 10-39. Head Line to Third Finger

Figure 10-40. Horizontal Head Line

The head line (Figure 10-39) that moves upward toward the third finger shows a tendency to seek immediate gratification. Unable to wait for personal satisfaction, the person wants his or her needs fulfilled quickly.

The upswing in Figure 10-40 denotes concern and worry about personal security, particularly in the areas of job, financial and family security. Fretting over security may increase the likelihood that the person becomes opportunistic.

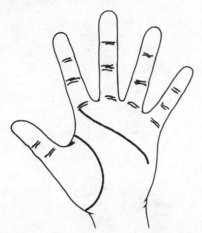

Figure 10-41. Self-Confident Head Line

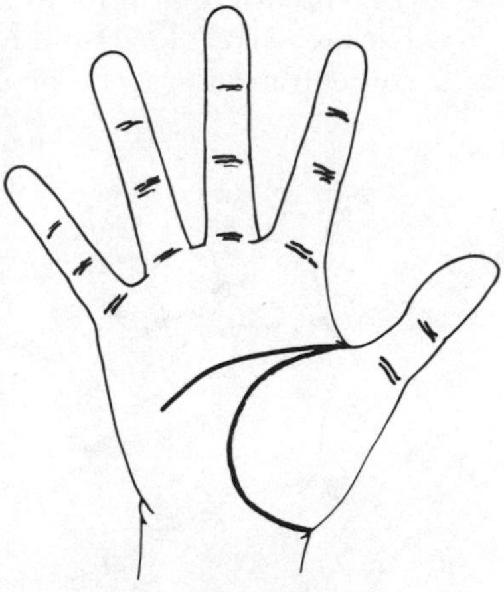

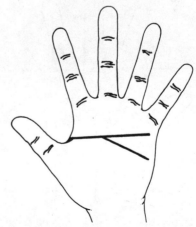

Figure 10-42. Head Line "Grounded" in Life Line

The head line which flows with the skin pattern, except for a slight curve upward toward the index finger (Figure 10-41), indicates a person with extraordinary self-confidence. Success in any endeavor is well assured, especially in positions of leadership and authority. Women with these lines tend to be successful in their careers.

The head line which is "grounded" in the life line (Figure 10-42) depicts a tendency to depend on others because of a lack of confidence and a cautious nature. This person tends to follow the dictates of convention, rather than risk anything novel.

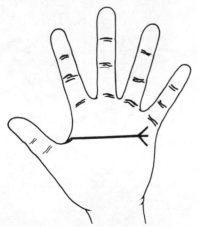

Figure 10-43. Horizontal Head Line with Arrow

Figure 10-44. Excessively Long Fork

A head line with a trident (Figure 10-43) is considered very favorable and can indicate a keen intelligence, flair for business, creative imagination or any combintion of the above.

The excessively long fork shown in Figure 10-44 indicates a tendency to lack concentration or to be single-minded.

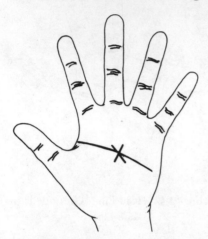

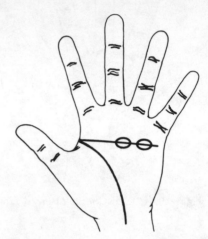

Figure 10-45. Cross on Head Line   Figure 10-46. Islands on Head Line

A cross on the head line (Figure 10-45) can mean there is a tendency toward self-deception. If it is found on a sloping line, it denotes a very serious nature.

Islands on the head line (Figure 10-46) generally reduce the ability to concentrate and weaken mental ability.

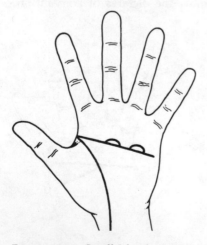

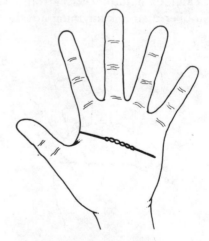

Figure 10-47. Small Islands on Head
Line

Figure 10-48. Chained Line

Small islands represent an area of mental confusion or indecision.

A chained line (Figure 10-48) shows a tendency toward indecision and even mental instability. This formation can reflect the need to improve concentration skills.

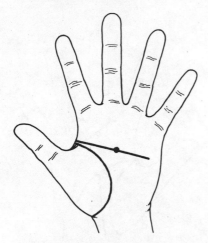

Figure 10-49. Dot on Head Line

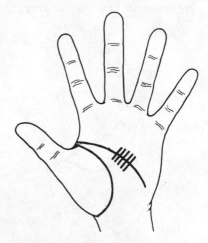

Figure 10-50. Lines Intersecting the Head Line

A dot on the head line (Figure 10-49) symbolizes that there has been an emotional shock or jolt to the system.

Lines intersecting the head line (Figure 10-50) can reflect a weakened ability to concentrate. It may also represent a tendency toward worrying, which frequently results in headaches.

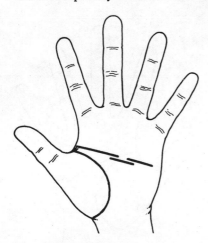

Figure 10-51. Sister Line

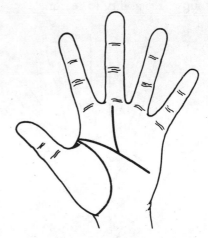

Figure 10-52. Split Head Line

A sister line (Figure 10-51) is a protective formation that serves to shelter an area of mental stress.

A formation with a second vertical line (Figure 10-52) is the head line of someone who can be distracted from their goals or even their work. They are prone to morbid thinking.

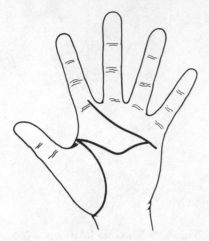

Figure 10-53. Head Line Overpowered by Heart Line

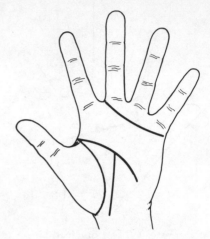

Figure 10-54. Fate Line Ends at Head Line

Sometimes the head line has been overpowered by the heart line (Figure 10-53). It represents someone who can easily be swayed by emotions, rather than logic.

When the fate line ends at the head line (Figure 10-54), feelings may upset the ability to reason.

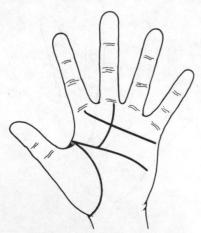

Figure 10-55. Passionate Head Line

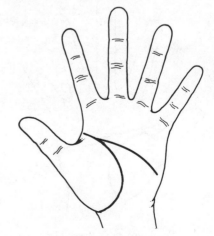

Figure 10-56. Head Line Connected to Life Line

If the head line splits and joins the heart line (Figure 10-55), a person whose reason is upset by passion is indicated.

When the head line is connected to the life line a short distance (Figure 10-56), it indicates a slow, cautious nature. The need for companionship is strong.

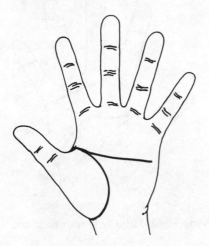

Figure 10-57. Horizontal Head Line
Connected to Life Line

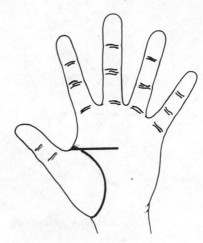

Figure 10-58. Short Head Line

Two lines that run together show someone who has overcome shyness (Figure 10-57).

A short head line (Figure 10-58) shows a lack of interest in intellectual pursuits.

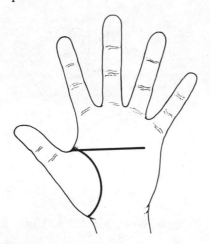

Figure 10-59. Flat Head Line

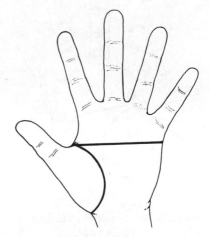

Figure 10-60. Full Head Line

A flat head line (Figure 10-59) shows that this person possesses at least an average intelligence.

A full head line (Figure 10-60)—a brilliant intellect!

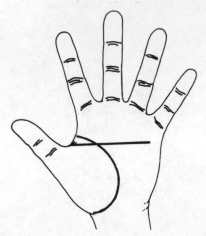

Figure 10-61. Head Line Intersecting
Life Line

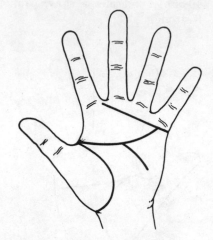

Figure 10-62. Head Line with Fork and
Support Line

A head line intersecting the life line (Figure 10-61) shows a person who has learned the art of self-control.

A head line with a fork and support line (Figure 10-62) belongs to someone who would sacrifice everything for the sake of love.

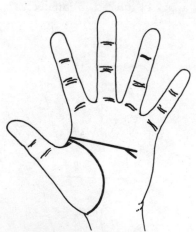

Figure 10-63. Small Fork at End of
Head Line

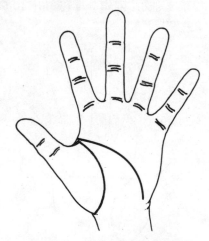

Figure 10-64. Sloped Head Line

The small fork at the end of the head line in Figure 10-63 shows imagination combined with common sense.

If the head line is slightly sloped or curved, as in Figure 10-64, the presence of imagination, sensitivity, and an artistic sense is indicated.

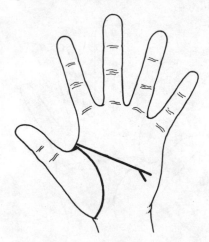

Figure 10-65. "Writer's Fork"

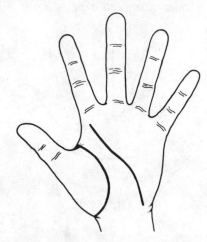

Figure 10-66. Politician's Head Line

Figure 10-65 shows the "writer's fork" and denotes a gift for self-expression, diplomacy and cleverness.

The next time you shake the hand of a politician, look at his or her head line—it may look like Figure 10-66.

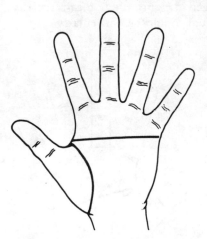

Figure 10-67. Long, Straight Head Line

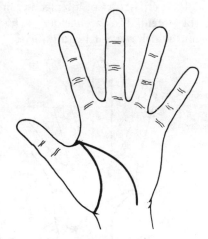

Figure 10-68. Downward Sloping Head Line

Figure 10-67 shows the long, straight head line of someone with a keen memory and persistence. This person is straight-forward, practical and realistic, but can also be selfish and calculating.

The head line shooting downward (Figure 10-68) can indicate a tendency toward depression or emotional love.

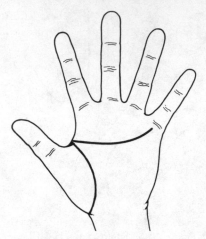

Figure 10-69. Upward Sloping Head
Line

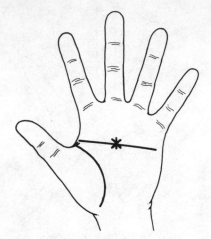

Figure 10-70. Intersecting Lines

The upward swing of the head line in Figure 10-69 depicts a preoccupation with money and material things.

A criss-cross of intersecting lines, as seen in Figure 10-70, means there is the potential for an accident. This individual should be particularly careful and watch out for head injuries.

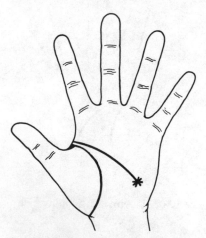

Figure 10-71. Intersecting Lines at End
of Head Line

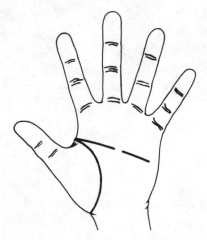

Figure 10-72. Break in Head Line

A criss-cross of intersecting lines at the end of the head line (Figure 10-71) depicts an unusual imagination, which could be developed. Others may interpret this exceptional imagination as being close to madness.

A break in the head line (Figure 10-72) means there is a possible danger to the brain.

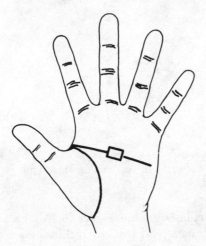

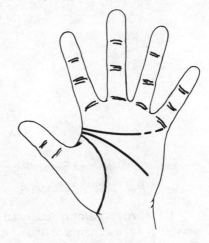

Figure 10-73. Break in Head Line with Square

Figure 10-74. Head Line Separate from Life Line

A break with a square (Figure 10-73) is an indication that there is some built-in protection.

If the head line is separate from the life line (Figure 10-74), it shows the presence of an independent nature, quick judgment, courage and enterprise. There is an ability to work alone with moderate success. The environment does not greatly influence this person since they live independently of it.

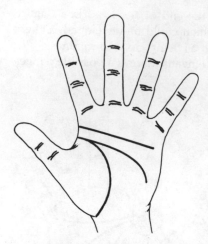

Figure 10-75. Wide Area Separating
Head and Heart Lines

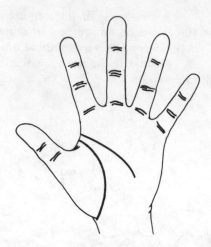

Figure 10-76. Sloping Head Line

If the area separating the head and heart lines is wide (Figure 10-75), the person is so independent that he or she may tend toward recklessness. Often, this person is impulsive, headstrong and rarely influenced by others.

If the head line slopes in a gentle curve (Figure 10-76), there is a tendency toward pessimism. This too, can be the hand commonly found on a politician or performer.

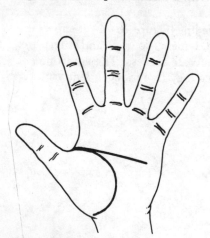

Figure 10-77. Merged Head and Life
Lines

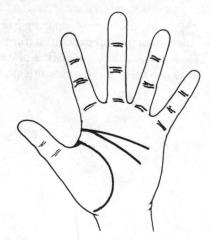

Figure 10-78. Convergence of Head and
Heart Lines

If the head and life lines merge for a great distance (Figure 10-77), it shows a degree of timidity. This person probably relies on the approval of others.

When the head and heart lines meet at the beginning (Figure 10-78) it denotes a cautious, conforming and cooperative individual who relies on others to inspire vitality.

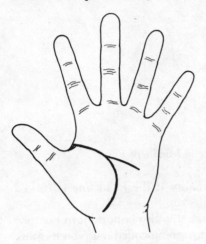

Figure 10-79. Head Line Emerges from Life Line

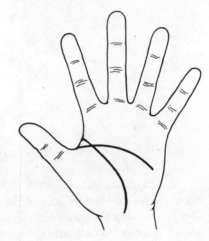

Figure 10-80. Head Line Intersects Life Line

If the head line starts from the life line (Figure 10-79), it indicates a person who depends on parents and family, and feels protected by them.

A head line that intersects the life line (Figure 10-80) shows a rebellious nature. This person can be fretful and touchy, and may have trouble controlling his or her temper.

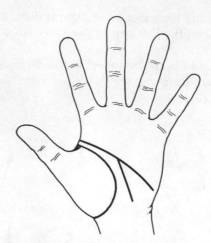

Figure 10-81. Forked Head Line in Middle of Palm

Figure 10-81 can depict a split personality if the head line is forked before it reaches the middle of the palm.

In assessing the meanings of various lines, it is also important to examine them in relation to each other. Therefore, it is recommended that you measure the distance between the end of the head line and the bottom of the life line. The closer the head line is, the greater the interrelationship between the mind and the nervous system. A head line in close proximity to the life line indicates quicker reaction to stimulus. It is fortunate to have a spread between the life and head line since it allows time to think before acting.

The Heart Line

This line is different from the head and the life lines in that it starts from the ulna side of the palm rather than the radial. This difference is significant because it carries information from the outer world (ulna side) in to the individual (radial side).

From the right hand, a stream of objective information from society about the person's value is brought in through the heart line. In the left hand, the person is brought messages of how others feel about her or him.

Unlike the head line, which is concerned with personal mental activity, or the life line, which is concerned with the inner personal vitality, the heart line is concerned with the *interrelationship* between the individual and the environment on which he or she depends.

The heart line begins under the little fingers on or just below the Mount of Mercury, which is the mount of communication with our environment. The line moves across the palm upward. The upward swing of the line represents the electrical power of energy, which naturally ascends.

The depth of the line indicates the amount you wish to receive from your environment. Shallow heart lines represent people who need little more than a bit of attention and occasional affection. Deep heart lines show greater expectations of others. The depth of the line also represents the person's emotional depth.

Generally, the length of the heart line denotes the length of your relationships and your ability to sustain them. Short heart lines represent a guarded person who generally prefers brief relationships. This person probably does not have a strong desire for intimacy and would rather do without the restrictions that relationships impose.

A shallow heart line, no matter how long, shows a tendency to be concerned with more superficial feelings. There is a tendency to avoid intense emotional attachments. Light-hearted flings are preferred instead.

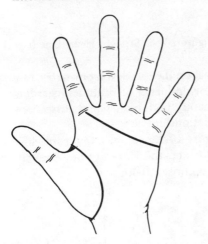 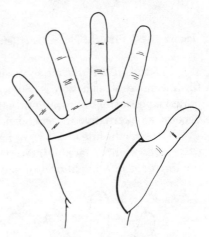

Figure 10-82. Long Heart Line (left) Figure 10-83. Long Heart Line (right)

The long heart line in Figure 10-82 represents how the outside world moves to shape and influence one's sense of personal power and worth. Positive input gives the energy for development of the index finger, which grows long. Likewise, negative input stunts the growth of the index finger and the person will feel less powerful and effectual. In the left hand, input creates an emotional self-image.

The ego is represented in the right hand (Figure 10-83). "We see ourselves as others see us," is the adage which best describes the process of the heart line. Positive reinforcement about physical prowess, health and power gives the individual impetus to develop physical strength.

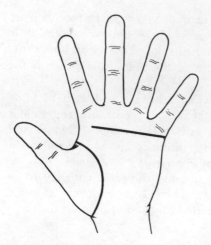
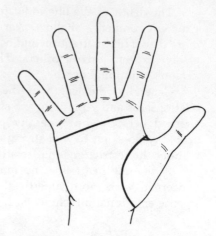

Figure 10-84. Straight Heart Line (left)   Figure 10-85. Straight Heart Line (right)

In Figure 10-84, the line shows little effect on the ego development because the line moves straight across. But it does show influence on attitudes regarding material possessions and values. In the left hand, food, money and possessions become an alternative to dependence on relationships.

The straight line of the right hand (Figure 10-85) can be a favorable sign since it represents a lack of interest in what others think about you. As such, the line depicts a likelihood of success in a chosen field.

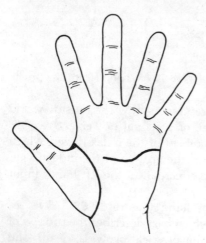
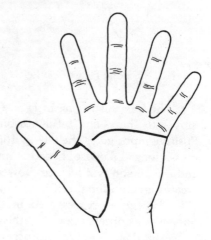

Figure 10-86. Heart Line Curved
Around Mount of Mercury

Figure 10-87. Descending Heart Line

A heart line that starts high and curves around the Mount of Mercury (Figure 10-86) reveals a taste for the occult and perhaps a talent for esoteric subjects and skills.

When the heart line starts to descend at the end rather than ascend (Figure 10-87), it shows that incoming energy is used for the pursuit of material pleasures and luxuries. These people can be quite possessive about their possessions or relationships.

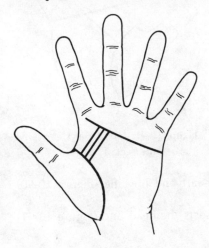

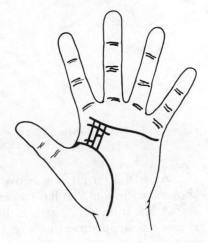

Figure 10-88. Lines Intersecting Head and Heart Lines

Figure 10-89. Conflict on Intersecting Lines

Lines that intersect the head and heart lines indicate the presence of parental affection (Figure 10-88).

The intersecting lines in Figure 10-89 represent the possibility of conflict within the parental relationships.

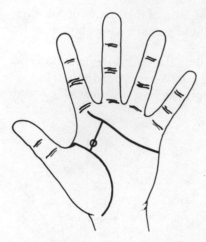

Figure 10-90. Island Between Heart and
Life Lines

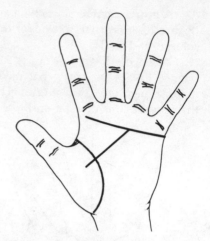

Figure 10-91. Line from Heart Line
Intersects Head Line

An island on the line between the heart and life line (Figure 10-90) shows a friendship that has caused pain.

A line from the heart line that intersects the head line (Figure 10-91) shows a disappointment in love.

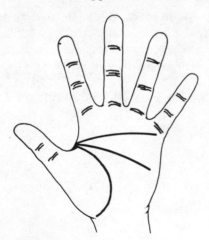

Figure 10-92. Double Heart Line

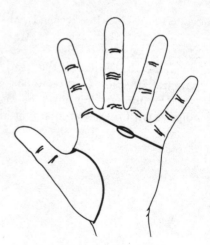

Figure 10-93. Island on Heart Line

Figure 10-92 denotes one who is apt to be hurt through love.

Figure 10-93 represents anxiety, a loss or emotional upset. It may possibly represent a physical ailment, also.

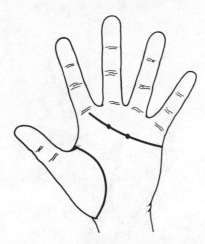

Figure 10-94. Dots on Heart Line

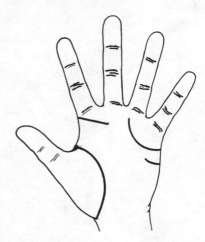

Figure 10-95. Gap in Heart Line

Figure 10-94 indicates an emotional shock.

A gap in the heart line represents a person who has difficulty staying in love since he or she tends to be fickle (Figure 10-95).

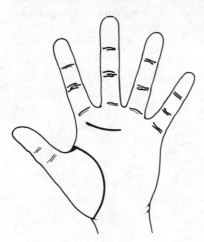

Figure 10-96. Short Heart Line Below
Middle Finger

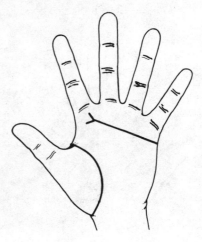

Figure 10-97. Small Fork at End of
Heart Line

A person with a short heart line below the middle finger should watch out for potential heart problems (Figure 10-96).

Figure 10-97 denotes harmony and happiness in marriage. In general, this person is tolerant, understanding and loyal.

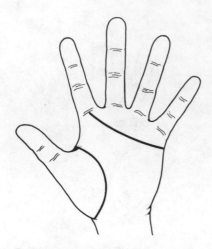

Figure 10-98. Heart Line Ending at
Index Finger

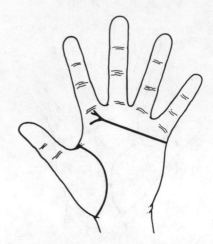

Finger 10-99. Three-Pronged Fork on
Heart Line

Figure 10-98 indicates a person ruled by pride and ambition. These individuals will marry well since they tend to be very discriminating.

Figure 10-99 indicates good luck and fine fortune, particularly in marriage.

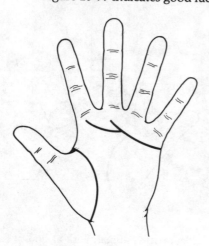

Figure 10-100. "Stop and Go" Heart
Line

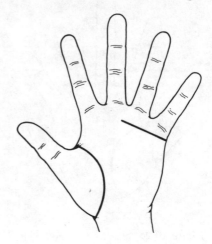

Figure 10-101. Incomplete Heart Line

Figure 10-100 shows the potential to be moody since this person has a mercurial nature.

Figure 10-101 represents a sensual person, but one who lacks true devotion and therefore is not likely to become a homebody.

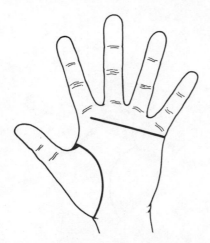

Figure 10-102. Deep Heart Line

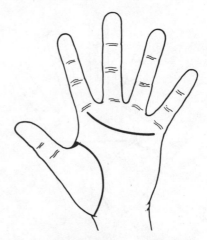

Figure 10-103. Heart Line with No
Beginning or End

If the heart line is high, long and deep (Figure 10-102), there is a great potential for possessiveness and even jealousy.

Figure 10-103 represents a lover. This person has great skill and luck at courting and lovemaking, but is less adept at achieving depth in relationships.

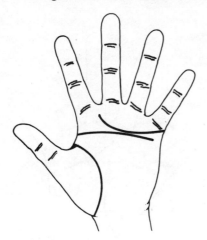

Figure 10-104. Heart Line Ruled by
Head Line

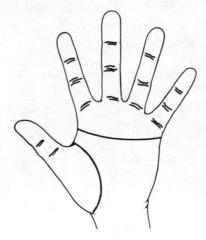

Figure 10-105. Heart and Life Lines
Separated in Left Hand

Figure 10-104 shows how the heart line is ruled by the head line, which prevents the emotions from flowing spontaneously.

If the heart and life line are joined in the right hand, but separated in the left hand (Figure 10-105), the person has difficulty compromising in his or her relationships. This person can appear ruthless and unemotional.

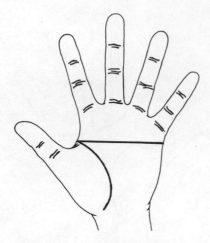

Figure 10-106. Heart and Life Lines
    Touch in Left Hand

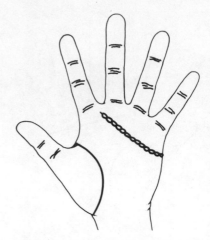

Figure 10-107. Chained Heart Line

If the heart and life line touch in the left hand only (Figure 10-106), it is likely that the person's mother was ill during her pregnancy and may have passed that condition to her child.

A chained heart line (Figure 10-107) can show a tendency toward fickleness or a mineral deficiency.

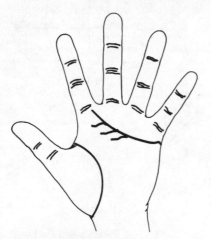

Figure 10-108. Lines off the Heart Line

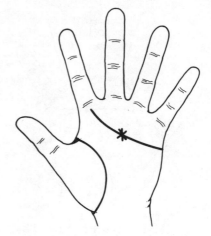

Figure 10-109. Criss-Cross on Heart
    Line

Lines off the heart line in Figure 10-108 show various disappointments.

A criss-cross of lines on the heart line shows a potential for heart problems in Figure 10-109.

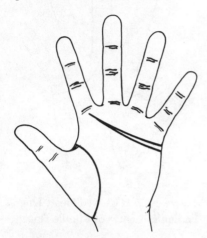

Figure 10-110. Sister Line

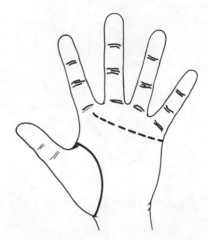

Figure 10-111. Breaks in Heart Line

A sister line (Figure 10-110) reinforces the qualities associated with the heart line.

A series of breaks in the heart line (Figure 10-111) depicts a potential for a weakening of the heart.

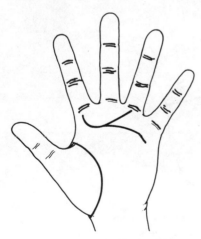

Figure 10-112. Split Heart Line

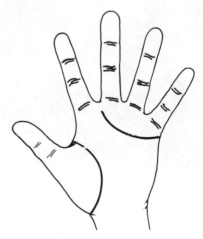

Figure 10-113. Curved Heart Line

Figure 10-112 denotes a person who has less emotional contact with those he or she loves than the person would like.

Figure 10-113 shows a romantic, tender-hearted and emotional lover.

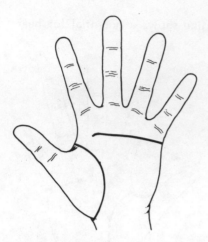

Figure 10-114. Straight Heart Line

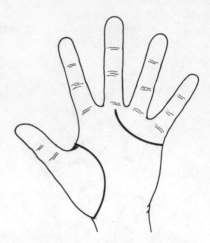

Figure 10-115. Curved Heart Line
Ending in Center of Middle Finger

A straight heart line (Figure 10-114) belongs to a person who is direct in his or her feelings and expresses them in a matter-of-fact way.

Figure 10-115 shows a cool calculator, especially in matters of love. This person is very shrewd about those he or she loves.

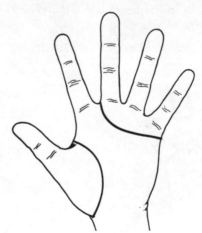

Figure 10-116. Curved Heart Line Ending
Between Index and Middle Fingers

Figure 10-116 represents a possessive person, but one who is also devoted to those he or she loves.

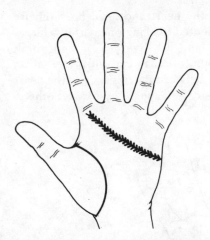

Figure 10-117. Feathered Heart Line

Figure 10-118. Partial, Double Heart Line

Figure 10-117 indicates a flirt, but this line also shows a person who is vivacious and dynamic.

Figure 10-118 represents someone who tends to be fickle. They find themselves on again, off again.

Introvert and Extrovert

Measure the space between the heart and head lines in the middle of both hands. The left hand determines whether you are instinctively introverted or extroverted. On the right hand, you will discover how you have developed as an introvert or extrovert. If your hands differ, your inner nature is in conflict with your outward actions.

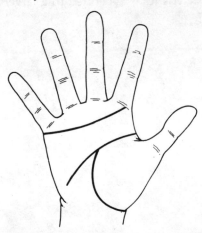

Figure 10-119. Great Distance Between Heart and Head Lines

If there is a great distance between the heart and head lines (Figure 10-119), you are an extrovert. You are oriented to being one within a larger whole. Your attitude is one of "live and let live." You can think impersonally about personal matters. Your concern over self-preservation is not very intense. If there is a wide space between the fingers and the heart line, it shows a great potential for generosity and sympathy toward others.

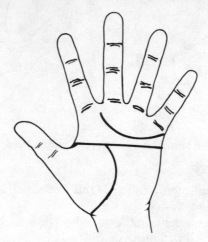

Figure 10-120. Short Distance Between
Heart and Head Lines

If the space between the heart and head lines is narrow (Figure 10-120), you are introverted and tend to be concerned with your self. You may often ask yourself, "What's in it for me?" Your preoccupation with self-preservation is intense. If this is found with a curved little finger, this represents these characteristics exaggerated to a larger degree.

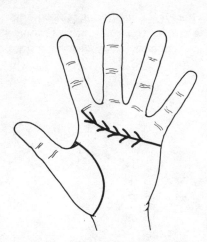

Figure 10-121. Feathered Heart Line

If found on both hands, feathering (Figure 10-121) indicates a person who tends to be fickle and whose affections fluctuate frequently. If the feathering droops downward, it shows a person who is frequently disappointed in personal relationships. If the feathering ascends upward, it shows an optimistic person who finds fulfillment in his or her relationships, even though the relationships may be brief.

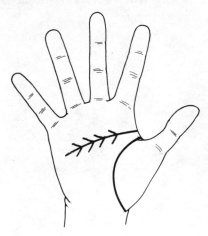

Figure 10-122. Feathered Head Line

Feathering on both sides of the head line (Figure 10-122) indicates indecisiveness. This person can't make up his or her mind to be either an optimist or a pessimist! If the feathering is only upward, it represents a belief that things must get better. If the feathering is drooping, it shows anxiety and apprehension about the future. This can mean a chronic state of tension. If the little finger is bent, these tendencies may become more pronounced.

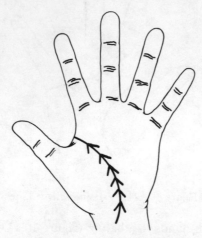

Figure 10-123. Feathered Life Line

A constant flux between retreating into a shell or making changes is seen when feathering occurs on both sides (Figure 10-123). Drooping on the inner side indicates a person who retreats from energetic activities. This person will prefer to stay at home.

11

Major and Minor Palm Lines

There is a second group of major lines, in addition to the life, heart and head lines. Unlike those lines, this second group is not found in every hand. There are four lines of the second major group—Jupiter, Saturn, Apollo and Mercury. Although these lines are not *necessary*, if any of them is present, it is certainly *significant*.

The four lines are named after the fingers under which they end. Generally, these lines begin near the wrist, traveling upward to meet one of the four fingers. These lines may begin elsewhere in the palm, though.

Jupiter. Lines that reach toward the finger of Jupiter, the index finger, are related to areas of self-achievement, independence and personal power. This is the finger of self-confidence.

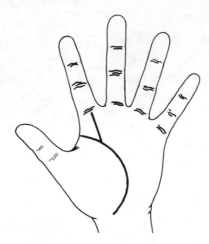

Figure 11-1. Jupiter Line

Saturn. Any lines that end below the middle finger, or the finger of Saturn, are considered fate lines. These lines are concerned with the person's fate as a social being and as a part of a group.

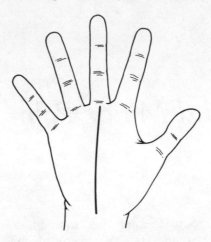

Figure 11-2. Saturn Line

Apollo. This line, which ends under the third finger, represents energy directed outward toward personal satisfaction (as opposed to social satisfaction). This line depicts activities that bring personal fulfillment and happiness to the individual. As such, they are sometimes referred to as happy lines or Sun lines. The lines of Apollo reveal the type of activities the individual is most naturally inclined to, and may even derive fame from. This line can be the strongest, clearest and longest of the four uprising lines.

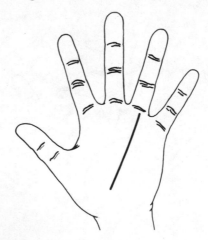

Figure 11-3. Apollo Line

Mercury. All the lines that end under the fourth finger relate to the person's relationship with the outside world and other people. This line usually originates low in the palm and is also called the health line or liver line. It indicates the person's state of health, as well as how others affect his or her health. The area of the lower palm represents the liver, which is the organ most directly affected by the influences of emotional relationships.

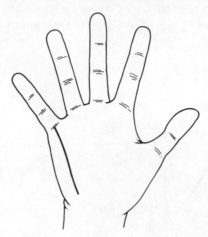

Figure 11-4. Mercury Line

Line of Jupiter

The line of Jupiter rises on the hand from the head line toward the index finger. It is frequently seen on the hands of self-made executives. That is, they have climbed the ladder of success through their own efforts. Sometimes it seems that the head line itself curves upward toward the index finger instead of going toward the thumb. This is a distinct mark of success in the world.

The Jupiter line could be called the line of personal ambition, for it denotes an innermost desire to succeed at all costs. Not to say the individual would be dishonest in any way, but the person is willing to work harder than the ordinary human being in order to become successful at their chosen career.

This is a rather unusual configuration and tends to be seen only on the most successful and self-made people. It almost invariably takes the configuration shown in Figure 11-1.

Saturn or Fate Line

The fate line is mainly concerned with the individual's material condition. The line represents the person's feelings of success in his or her evironment, particularly in financial areas. Generally, if the line is clear and straight, it means the person is inwardly content and satisfied; however, if the line is split or fading, dissatisfaction is indicated. This is the line in which a person's satisfaction with material success or status is reflected.

The fate line is the most flexible of the lines and subject to quick changes, depending on the state of personal satisfaction. If a person's satisfaction with his or her lot increases or decreases, this change will be quickly reflected in the fate line. Crosses on a fate line or a chained fate line show difficult periods. An island depicts a period of uncertainty.

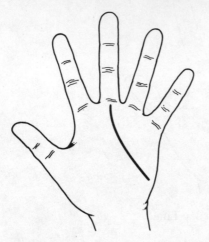

Figure 11-5. Saturn Line Curving Away
from Thumb

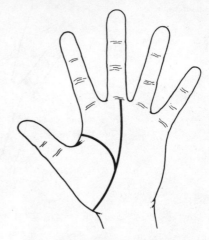

Figure 11-6. Split Fate Line

Dependence on other people for success is shown in a long, curved line (Figure 11-5). Personal satisfaction depends on public opinion and others' approval.

A split line (Figure 11-6) indicates restrictive circumstances that hampered personal satisfaction in early years. These limitations were beyond the control of the individual.

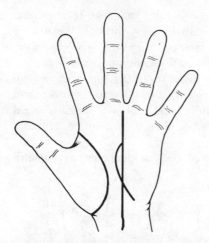

Figure 11-7. Influence Line Attached to
Fate Line

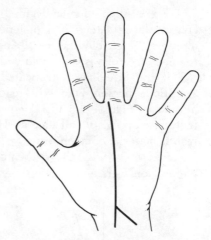

Figure 11-8. Forked Fate Line

Figure 11-7 depicts an influence line attached to a fate line. The influence line in this case is one of affection and indicates a point of union, generally marriage. If the influence line crosses over the fate line, opposition to the union is in evidence. If an island is apparent at the intersection of the fate and influence lines, difficulties may follow because of divided or ambivalent feelings.

Figure 11-8 denotes an early marriage, which serves as a career because of material considerations.

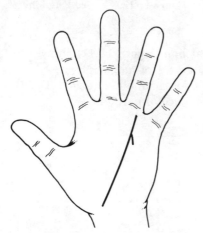

Figure 11-9. Line of Affection Joins
Line of Apollo

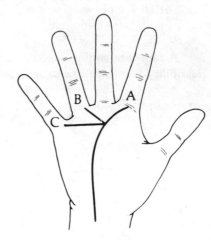

Figure 11-10. Fate Line Reaching to
Various Fingers

The configuration in Figure 11-9 shows a later marriage for personal considerations rather than material. This can be seen through the line of affection, which joins the line of Apollo at a later point on the line. (Remember, the line of Apollo is concerned with personal satisfaction and happiness.)

If the fate line is truncated, as in Figure 11-10 (A), it shows an ambitious person who will reach a position of influence, power and authority. Figure 11-10 (B) depicts an individual who will possess good fortune, popularity and success. He or she will gain public notice, and as a result, material compensation.

Figure 11-10 (C) shows the possibility of great achievement and wealth from a commercial or scientific endeavor.

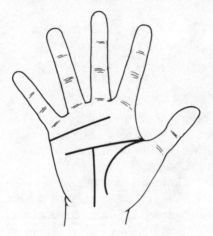

Figure 11-11. Capped and Truncated Fate Line

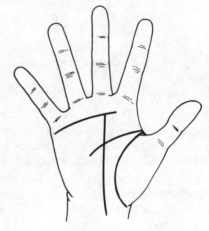

Figure 11-12. Capped Fate Line

A fate line ending under a horizontal line (Figure 11-11) shows the possibility of misfortune or loss through an error of judgment.

If the fate line crosses one line and ends at another (Figure 11-12), personal progress may be hampered by a choice of partners.

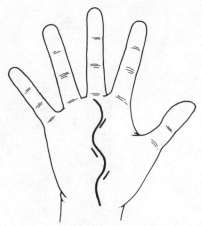

Figure 11-13. Wavy Fate Line

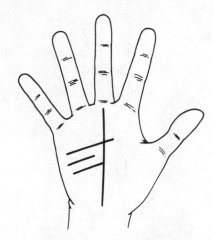

Figure 11-14. Influence Lines

Figure 11-13 indicates a person who is either quarrelsome, mercurial or disorganized.

Each influence crossing the fate line (Figure 11-14) carries its own significance. The bottom line shows a marriage. The second line depicts a marriage that was planned, but broken off. The top line shows a marriage that ended in separation or divorce.

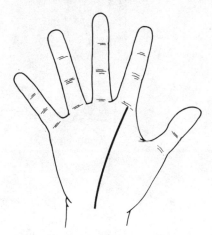

Figure 11-15. Line of Public Success

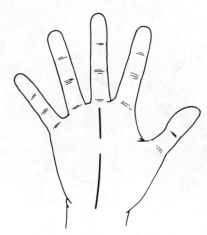

Figure 11-16. Gap in Fate Line

Public success is indicated when the fate line curves to the index finger (Figure 11-15). A break in the line in Figure 11-16 shows the possibility of a business loss.

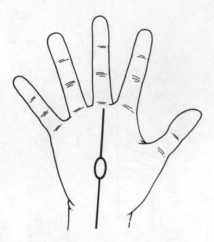

Figure 11-17. Island on Fate Line

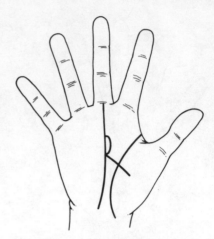

Figure 11-18. Island and Secondary
Lines off Fate Line

Figure 11-17 indicates the possibility of a career loss due to a poor public reputation.

The formation in Figure 11-18, which is similar to Figure 11-17, shows evidence of a situation that could become scandalous.

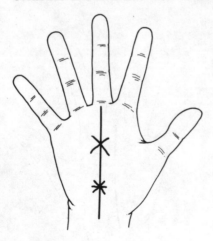

Figure 11-19. Stars and Crosses

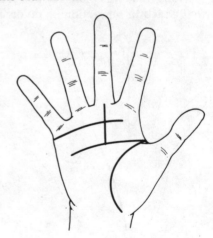

Figure 11-20. Fate Line Beginning in
Middle of Hand

Figure 11-19 depicts the possible misfortune of someone close to you.

Figure 11-20 indicates success beginning in midlife that is due to personal perseverance.

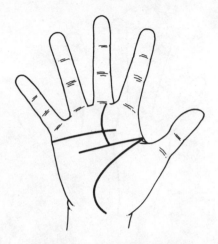

Figure 11-21. Curved Fate Line
Beginning in Middle of Hand

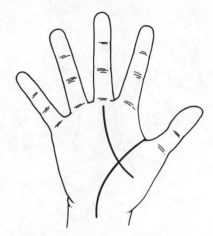

Figure 11-22. Curved Fate Line

Figure 11-21 shows later success, but there are more struggles to overcome first.

Figure 11-22 shows that the person was controlled by the family early in life, but success comes later on. The career is probably the result of action by relatives who give the person a start.

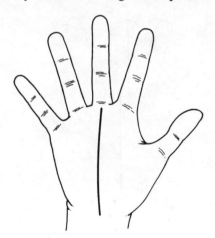

Figure 11-23. Full Fate Line

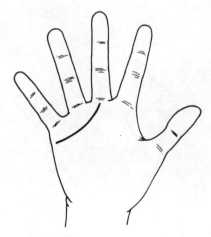

Figure 11-24. Fate Line Curving Away
from Thumb

Figure 11-23 shows a life of security, as well as much happiness. A successful career is also indicated.

Figure 11-24 shows a strong personal effort to achieve security.

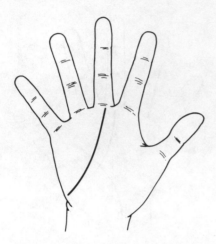

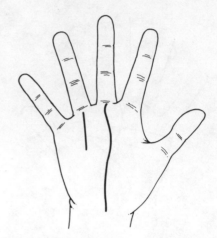

Figure 11-25. Fate Line Curving Low
on Hand

Figure 11-26. Fate Line with Partial
Complement

Figure 11-25 means success and depends on opportunities from others. This line is particularly linked with travel, change or variety.

Figure 11-26 denotes a colorful, successful life, perhaps connected with the artistic realm.

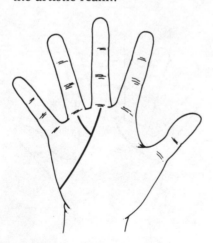

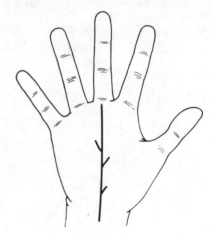

Figure 11-27. Partnership Lines

Figure 11-28. Lines of Ambition

Figure 11-27 shows the joining together of a partnership.

The upward featherings in Figure 11-28 are lines of ambition.

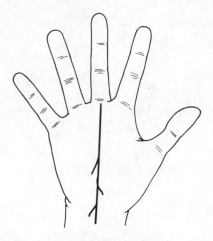

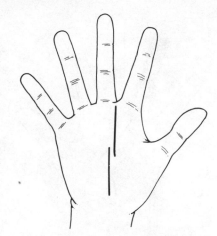

Figure 11-29. Lines of Failed Efforts   Figure 11-30. Broken Fate Line

Likewise, the downward featherings in Figure 11-29 are efforts gone askew.

The breaks in Figure 11-30 indicate that a change is in store.

Apollo Line

The line of Apollo is also known as the Sun line, the line of success, fame or brilliance—all areas with which this line is concerned. It always points to the third finger. If it is well-marked, clear, deep, straight and originating near the Neptune mount, it shows a magnetic personality, success, and the opportunity to maximize personal talents. Fortune smiles on these individuals, bringing them fame and success in their chosen field.

An excellent Apollo line shows brilliance in achievement. A strong Apollo line and a curving head line (indicating imagination) suggest the development of the person's artistic nature. If the head line is deep and straight, and the Apollo line is strong, success in the material world is likely.

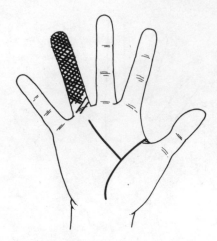

Figure 11-31. Crosses on Apollo
Finger

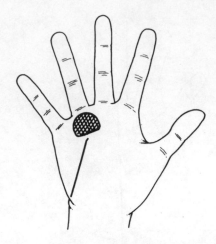

Figure 11-32. Crosses on Mount of
Apollo

Figure 11-31 shows a person who is successfully dedicated to the arts.
Figure 11-32 shows a creative personality who can achieve public acclaim.

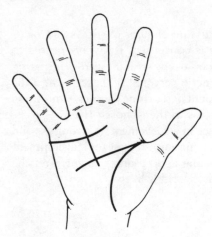

Figure 11-33. Apollo Line Crossed by
Other Lines

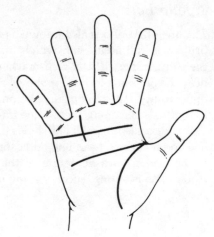

Figure 11-34. Apollo Line Starting from
Horizontal Line

Figure 11-33 indicates that success is seen after age thirty because of personal efforts.

Figure 11-34 shows self-sufficiency in old age, as well as good taste and good fortune in marriage.

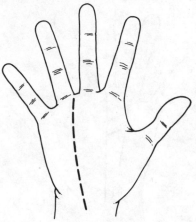

Figure 11-35. Broken Apollo Line

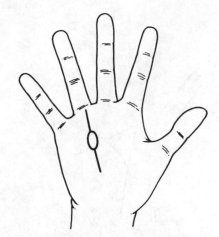

Figure 11-36. Island

Figure 11-35 suggests much versatility. However, this person's eccentric ideas can cause difficulty.

The person with an island (Figure 11-36) should be careful to protect his or her reputation.

Figure 11-37. Star

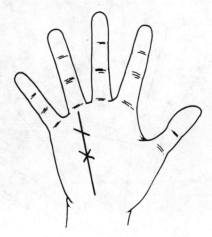

Figure 11-38. Cross-Bar

Figure 11-37 indicates a brilliant success!

The cross-bar and cross of Figure 11-38 indicate obstacles or a possible poor reputation.

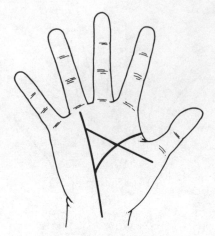

Figure 11-39. Apollo Line As Part of
Large Triangle

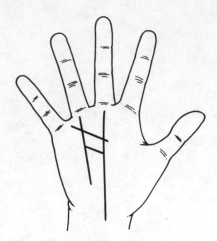

Figure 11-40. Bottom and Top
Influence Lines

Figure 11-39 suggests that money will be gained by friends or family.
The bottom influence line of Figure 11-40 depicts a successful
partnership while the top line shows a partnership that could falter.

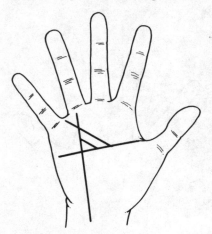

Figure 11-41. Bottom and Top
Influence Lines

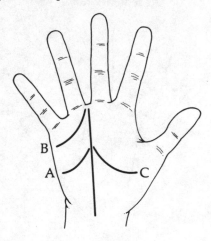

Figure 11-42. Curved Influence Lines

The bottom influence line in Figure 11-41 shows that money was gained
due to cleverness, but the top influence line shows that money was lost due
to foolishness.

The influence lines in Figure 11-42 marked A shows that a legacy can be
expected. In B, the inheritance will be a surprise, while in C, property or
money will be left behind by relatives.

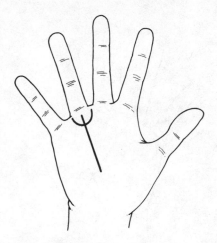

Figure 11-43. Trident

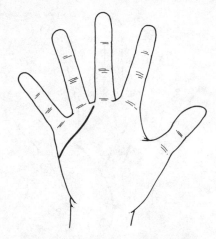

Figure 11-44. Apollo Line Curving
to Ulnar Side

Figure 11-43 depicts a trident, which guarantees wealth, achievement and social acclaim.

Figure 11-44 indicates that success is gained through personal efforts.

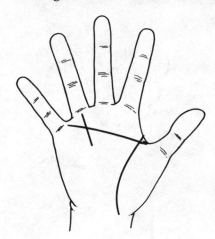

Figure 11-45. Crossed Apollo Line

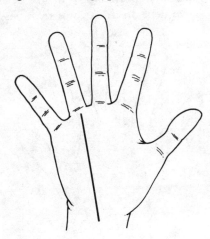

Figure 11-46. Ideal Apollo Line

A short Apollo line crossed by another line (Figure 11-45) means the person can be influenced by an enemy.

A long straight line (Figure 11-46) is the *ideal* Apollo line, bringing the best of fame, achievement and brilliance.

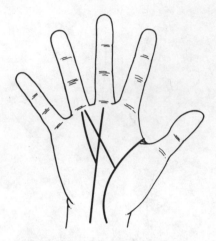

Figure 11-47. Multiple Apollo Lines

Figure 11-48. Long Apollo Line

Figure 11-47 suggests that success is due to the person's own qualities, or persistence.

Figure 11-48 suggests a sensitive person—one aware of beauty and harmony, particularly in art or literature. However, he or she may be dependent on the help of relatives.

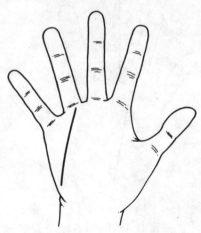

Figure 11-49. Long Apollo Line
Reaching for Ulnar Side

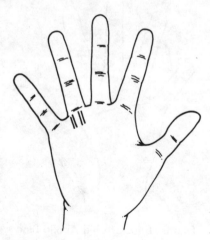

Figure 11-50. Jack-of-All-Trades Line

In Figure 11-49, success is dependent on the favor of the opposite sex, and there is good potential for fortune, wealth and fame.

Figure 11-50 shows a jack-of-all-trades, master-of-none.

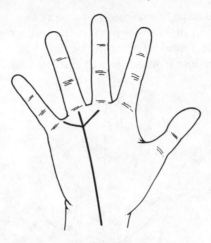

Figure 11-51. Trident on Apollo Line

A long line ending in a trident (Figure 11-51) is the line of a celebrity, whose success is based on a solid, lasting foundation.

Mercury Line

This line is also referred to as the Health Line, the Hepatica, Spleen Line or the Liver Line. In particular, it represents our state of health and digestion. People who lack this line usually enjoy an active healthy digestive system for the outer world does not adversely affect their inner condition.

The health line stops at the heart line or below. Any lines beyond the heart line are considered Empathy Lines. When the health line is flawed, frayed or broken, it indicates irritation, anger, hastiness, impatience or confusion.

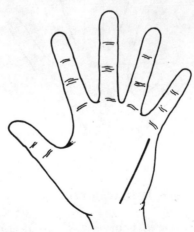

Figure 11-52. Straight Health Line

A straight, deep and clear line (Figure 11-52) on either hand shows excellent health due to a strong digestive system in the liver (represented in the left hand) and the spleen (found reflected in the right hand). This person enjoys good health and freedom from anxiety and worry, so therefore is energetic and optimistic.

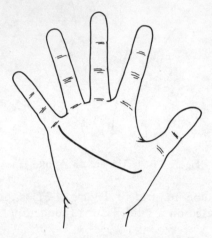

Figure 11-53. Health Line Curved Toward Thumb

Figure 11-53 shows a tendency toward nervous tension, poor digestion, and acidity from conscious worry (reflected in the right hand) and/or inner anxiety (represented in the left hand).

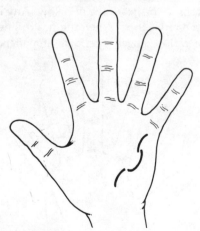

Figure 11-54. Curled Health Line

A broken Mercury line that curves back on itself shows a person who has difficulty releasing worry or anxiety and can be prone to attacks of indigestion. These individuals allow themselves to be consumed with negative thoughts, represented in the right hand, or overwhelmed with negative feelings, reflected in the left hand.

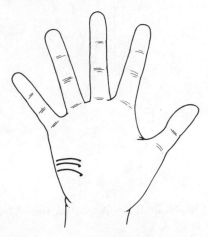

Figure 11-55. Horizontal Health Lines

Figure 11-55 shows the right hand, with short curved lines that indicate stress on the spleen due to conflicts with authority or those who have power over the individual.

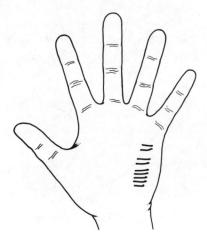

Figure 11-56. Multiple Horizontal Health Lines

Figure 11-56 depicts the left hand, with similar marks that show inner tension and anxiety that can cause digestive problems if they are not addressed. This can be evidence of conflict between subjective feelings and objective beliefs and attitudes.

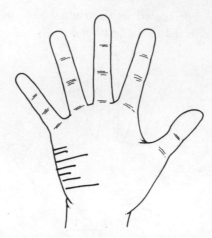

Figure 11-57. Health Lines Appearing from Ulnar Side

Figure 11-57 shows some horizontal lines are longer than others. Stress on both the liver and spleen is a possibility. The stress can be the result of difficulties in emotional attachments and relationships to power figures.

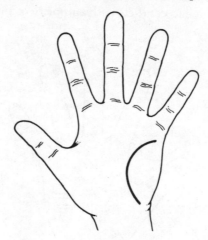

Figure 11-58. Line of Rapport

Figure 11-58 depicts a line that curves outward at its beginning and end. This is the line of rapport with the outer world, represented in the right hand, and rapport with the psychic world, as reflected in the left hand. It depicts great sensitivity and consideration to the feelings and thoughts of others.

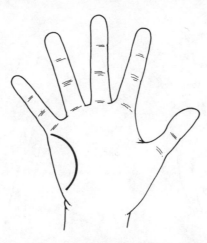

Figure 11-59. Outward Curved Health Line

When both hands have the line depicted in Figure 11-59, both the subjective and objective consciousness are equally aware. These lines are always curved at the top, but not necessarily at the bottom.

Minor Lines Modifying the Line of Health

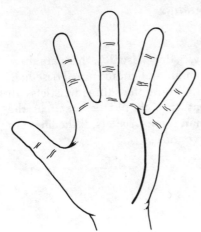

Figure 11-60. Business Line

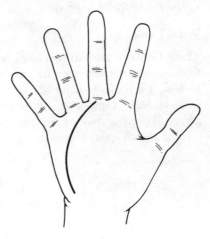

Figure 11-61. Hard-Working Line

Figure 11-60 shows success through a shrewd business nature.

Figure 11-61 shows that success can be achieved through hard work, sobriety and far-sightedness.

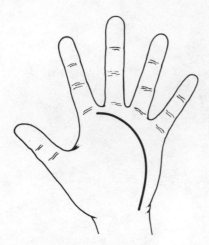

Figure 11-62. Executive Line

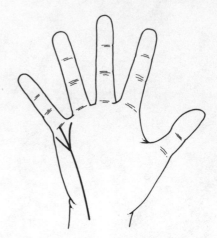

Figure 11-63. Stable Line

Figure 11-62 suggests a talented executive with the likelihood of a very successful business career.

Figure 11-63 suggests an extremely well-balanced and stable person. This individual probably enjoys great health.

Other Minor Lines or Lines of Influence

Wrist Lines

These lines are also known as rascettes or wristlets. Usually, there are three that circle the wrist, denoting physical strength and endurance. These help to ensure a long, healthy life and if there are more than three wristlets, an exceptionally long life is indicated. Great care should be taken of the physical body, however, if there are less than three wristlets. If the lines are strong and deep, it shows a life full of adventure.

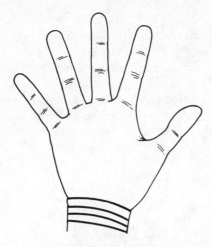

Figure 11-64A. Humped Wristlets

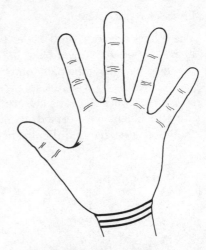

Figure 11-64B. Humped Wristlets

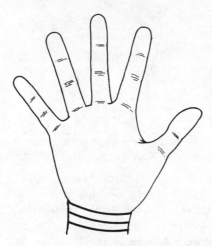

Figure 11-64C. Humped Wristlets

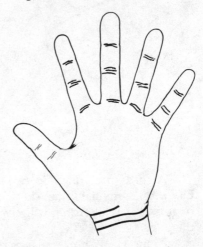

Figure 11-65. Broken Wristlet

These formations of Figure 11-64 A, B, and C are found in both men and women. Humped wristlets show a love of children and a desire to have them. In women, this tendency is particularly strong, and the needs of the children will always come first. Women with many curved wristlets show a desire for a large family.

In women, a broken wristlet (Figure 11-65) can signal potential problems with the first pregnancy due to reproductive abnormalities. Sometimes, the first pregnancy can end in a miscarriage, although if the pregnancy is carried full term, it will eliminate the problem for future pregnancies.

Lines of Attachment

These lines are found just under the little finger running horizontally. These lines may stretch toward the back side of the hand. A good palm print, obtained by rolling the palm onto the ulna side, will reveal these lines clearly.

Generally, these lines represent deep emotional relationships and sometimes marriage. The closer they are to the heart line, the earlier in life the attachment was formed. If the line begins in a fork on the back side of the hand, it suggests difficulty in the early stages of the relationship.

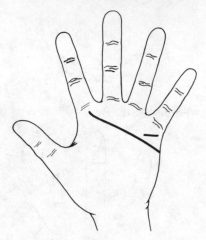

Figure 11-66. Single, Deep Line of
Attachment

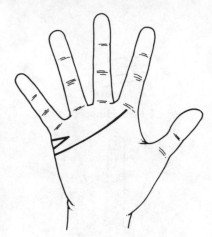

Figure 11-67. Line of Emotional
Difficulty

A single deep line (Figure 11-66) denotes one significant relationship. Likewise, many light lines show many less serious relationships. The depth or length of relationship will always be reflected in the depth or length of the line.

Figure 11-67 shows delay and frustration before marriage. It shows the possibility of difficulty at the beginning of an emotional relationship.

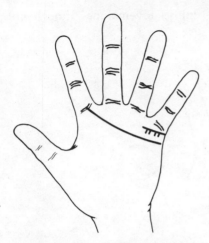

Figure 11-68. Line of Anxiety

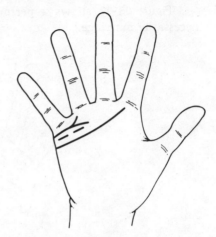

Figure 11-69. Attachment Line with Fork

The lines depicted in Figure 11-68 show anxiety or financial worries connected to a marriage or love affair.

Figure 11-69 shows a relationship that starts off well but eventually each person will go their separate ways.

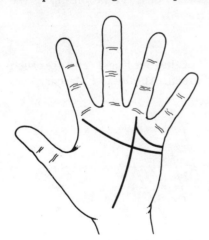

Figure 11-70. Curved Line of Attachment

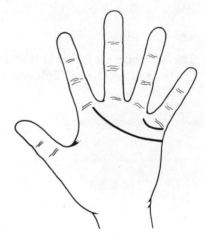

Figure 11-71. Partial, Double Line of Attachment

If the line of attachment curves up and touches the line of the Sun (Apollo), a brilliant marriage is likely (Figure 11-70). However, if the line cuts through the Sun line, it may jeopardize happiness.

Figure 11-71 shows a person who enjoys lovemaking, though not necessarily marriage.

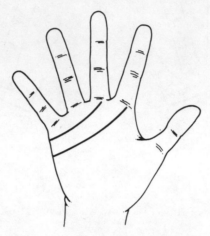

Figure 11-72. Long Line of Attachment Pointing to Saturn

A long line of attachment which points to the Saturn finger denotes a karmic tie with your mate (Figure 11-72), possibly from a past life. Check the beginning of this line to determine the start of this relationship. Is the line smooth and straight, or broken and frayed?

The Four Rings

The four rings are found at the base of each of the four fingers and are called the rings of Jupiter (or Solomon's ring), Saturn, Apollo and Mercury.

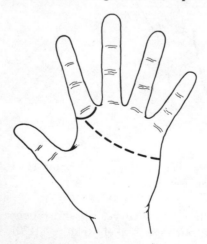

Figure 11-73. Ring of Jupiter

The ring of Jupiter (Figure 11-73) denotes a very sympathetic individual who may be a fine teacher or therapist. This is a rare marking and speaks of an individual of unusual wisdom. These people may have a potential or actual activity in the psychic realm. In addition, they know how to exercise power and authority wisely.

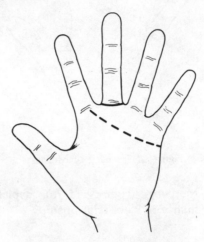

Figure 11-74. Ring of Saturn

The ring of Saturn (Figure 11-74) indicates a tendency toward depression, morbidity and melancholy. These people tend to possess a pessimistic outlook of the world.

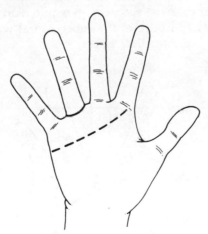

Figure 11-75. Ring of Apollo

The ring of Apollo (Figure 11-75) shows an enthusiastic and bubbly vitality. This person loves a good time and pleasurable activities.

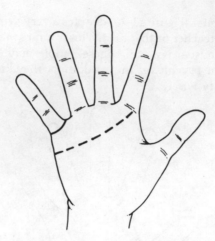

Figure 11-76. Ring of Mercury

The ring of Mercury (Figure 11-76) depicts an exceptional communicator, particularly in close relationships.

The Mystic Cross

The cross is found in a variety of forms, but is always connected with the heart and head lines at four points. It represents great psychic power, depicted in the incoming forces of energy joined to the head line. If placed under the index finger, it reflects uncanny insight into the minds and motivations of others. If it is found in the right hand, business success is likely. In the left hand, social success is possible. Fortune tellers, psychic readers, ghost stories and tales of the supernatural will be enjoyed by a person with a cross under the little finger.

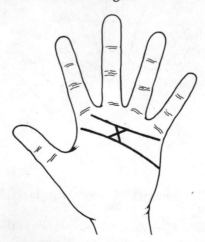

.gure 11-77. The Mystic Cross

St. Joseph's Cross

This cross is found attached between the life line and the line of Saturn. This person is courageous and is likely to be a peace advocate or activist. Ambulance drivers in war are likely examples of persons with this type of cross. Peace marchers, anti-nuke supporters and all those who support peace and abhor conflict are also likely to have this cross. The cross is actually composed of two lines—a line of sympathy for others and a "travel line" showing a willingness to leave home for the sake of others.

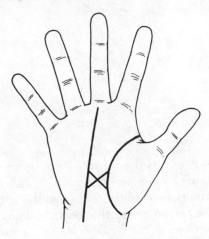

Figure 11-78. St. Joseph's Cross

The Line of Mars

This line depicts vigor and strength in an otherwise weak life line. It protects the person's life, particularly if the life line is delicate, lacking in depth or width. This line is also called the parent line because it often indicates the presence of a parent who is strong, resistant to outer influence and who has raised his or her children with similar traits. The strength of this line also gives resistance to disease and harmful bacteria. A person with this line will most likely recover quickly from physical stress, emotional duress or illness.

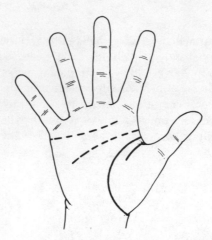

Figure 11-79. Line of Mars

The Girdle of Venus

Usually composed of two lines that "girdle" the Saturn and Apollo fingers, this formation shows extreme sensitivity and keen perception. Occasionally, the two lines are joined, although this is rare. If this is found on the right hand, the person gives off an electrical quality that others will feel as radiance. Likewise, if the girdle is apparent on the left hand, this person will have a magnetic nature that will draw others to him or her. A person who has the girdle on both hands is likely to be a vital, sensuous person with a sensual appeal to others. However, these qualities can become exaggerated and extreme if the girdle is complete and unbroken, indicating an obsessive sensual nature.

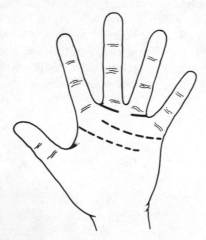

Figure 11-80. Girdle of Venus

The Via Lascivia

This line, which starts on the outer edge of the palm and crosses the area which represents the spleen, generally shows a bodily response to that which is ingested from the outside. For example, this line may indicate an allergy or a destructive appetite. These conditions are a reflection of either emotional intolerance, if the line is found in the left hand, or mental intolerance, if the line is found in the right hand. The body "acts out" (in a physical manifestation like obesity or an allergic rash) to show resistance to an adverse outside influence, such as food or an allergic substance. If such oppressing conditions persist, the spleen might also become permanently enlarged and further endanger health.

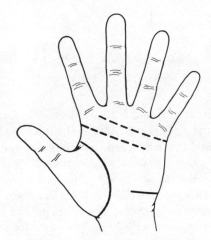

Figure 11-81. The Via Lascivia (Allergy Line)

Family Line

The family line is found at the base of the second thumb phalange. This line is usually chained, which is a favorable characteristic showing a strong sense of family. If the family line extends straight up and down when the palm is outstretched, the person is capable of universal love and feels kinship with all humankind. However, this sense of kinship is limited to the immediate blood relations, if the line curls protectively around the thumb. If the line is present, but singular, rather than chained, then the person lacks a feeling of unity with his or her family.

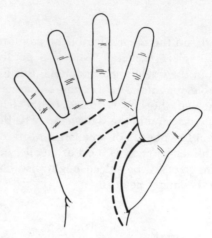

Figure 11-82. The Family Line

Empathy Lines

These lines should not be confused with children's lines, although both these lines are found on the Mount of Mercury. Empathy lines always begin above the heart line and move upward, whereas children's lines originate at the crease of the little finger and move downward.

Empathy lines, as the name implies, represent a person who is capable of sympathy with all those *unlike* him- or herself. Anyone in a social service profession would benefit from them. These people are particularly helpful and compassionate to anyone in distress. The capacity to become a psychic healer is indicated, although it may not be actually acted upon.

Also called the Medical Stigmatic lines, these lines show a particular aptitude for caring for the sick and aged with skill and empathy. A doctor without them would perhaps be better suited as a surgeon, where a bedside manner is not as vital.

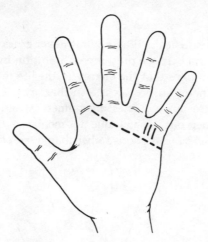

Figure 11-83. Empathy Lines

Children's Lines

Children's lines suggest a keen aptitude for relating to children either as a parent, teacher, or child psychologist. These people are successful with children because they feel a special, and often deep, empathy for very young people. A child with these lines will forever keep the awareness of his or her childhood, so as to better relate to children the rest of his or her life.

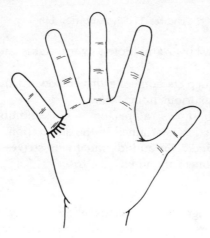

Figure 11-84. Children's Lines

Ambition Lines

These lines always begin at the life line, but never cross it. They are strong, straight lines which indicate the presence of ambition in whatever direction they point to. This implies that the energy of the life line is funneled into a particular goal and helps ensure success in that area.

However, if these upward lines are numerous and tiny, it indicates a breakdown in the nervous system due to mental difficulties. These lines represent efforts to escape restrictions rather than attempts to overcome them.

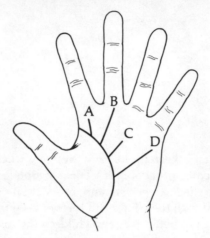

Figures 11-85. Ambition Lines

Figure 11-85A shows ambition toward status and career success is evident.

Figure 11-85B depicts someone driven toward material possessions, such as money, a luxurious home, etc.

Figure 11-85C shows a person with ambitions for fame and recognition. Satisfaction is attained in the admiration of others.

Figure 11-85D indicates an individual who strives in fields of business or science and is monetarily ambitious, too.

Anxiety Lines

When our needs are ignored or unsatisfied, we worry. When the worry is ineffective, we become anxious, expending much energy, which marks the hand with anxiety lines. All anxiety lines point to the areas where we desperately attempt to fill the needs that have not been fulfilled by others.

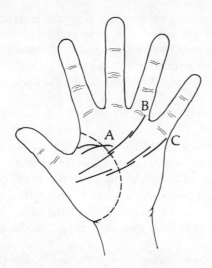

Figure 11-86A. Line of Family Anxiety. B. Line of Close Friendships.
C. Line of Financial Security

Figure 11-86A shows lines of anxiety caused by the family.

Figure 11-86B shows a need to be socially accepted and liked. Here, great efforts are made to get praise and personal satisfaction through friends.

Figure 11-86C shows a need for financial and material security, and is usually achieved with lines this strong. It cuts across all lines of sympathy and brooks no interference.

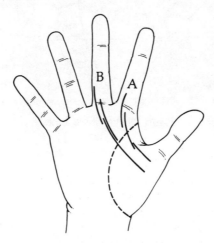

Figure 11-87A. Line of Personal Recognition. B. Line of Divided Anxiety

Figure 11-87A shows a need to be recognized and feel success. If the line is strong, the person will often reap fame and recognition.

Figure 11-87B shows tremendous energy divided between a successful home, a family to be proud of and a career to boast about. These lines can affect the heart lines so these people should watch for heart problems due to overwork.

Stress Lines

Lines along the outer edge of the palm show stress that the individual suffers. The stress is caused by outside influences and conflicts. Stress lines along the upper area of the palm show stress to the liver, as a result of emotional dissappointments, or feelings of rejection and alienation. Stress lines along the lower palm area show problems with the spleen, caused by concerns about job security, finances, social conflicts or acceptance of social roles.

If the person lives in harmony with the world, the palm will be clear of stress lines, showing an energy field which is active and receptive. This person is responsive to the world, but not in conflict with it.

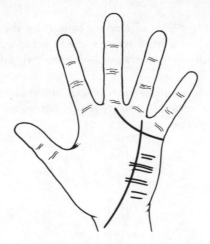

Figure 11-88. Stress Lines

Influence Lines

There are several types of these lines, which denote different kinds of influences, but all are found on the Mount of Venus. Generally, they are related to the influence of other people on the individual. Faint lines show lesser influence, deep lines denote heavy influence. If only a few, heavy lines are present, the person has had only a few, close relationships. A Mount of Venus with many fine lines indicates the presence of many friends and acquaintances. If all the lines are contained within the life line without crossing it, then the relationships have not changed your life. However, if the lines extend beyond the life line, the relationships have influenced the course of your life. Influence lines also tell of the need for affection, attention and friends.

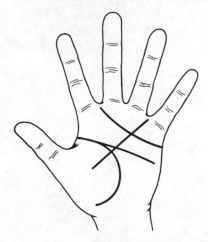

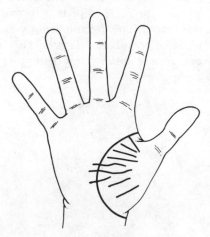

Figure 11-89. Long-Lasting Influence Line

Figure 11-90. Multiple Influence Lines

Figure 11-89 denotes a strong, deep and long-lasting relationship, which has had a vast influence on the individual.

Figure 11-90 depicts a person who has numerous relationships, some of which have greatly changed the outcome of the person's life.

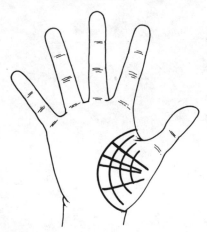

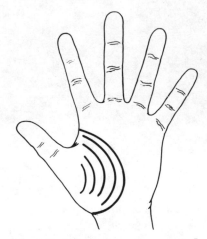

Figure 11-91. Lines of Many Friendships

Figure 11-92. Lines of Resistance to Influence

The lines in Figure 11-91 picture a person who has many friends and affections, but does not allow them to change his or her lifestyle or personal environment. A gregarious, affectionate person is seen here. This person feels secure enough to gather many friends and lovers.

Figure 11-92 depicts a formation that indicates a resistance to being influenced. This person is not very suggestible and dislikes being told what to do by friends or relatives. This resistance also applies to health, since the person is immune from many diseases.

12

The Mounts

The palm is sometimes called the "flat of the hand," but this phrase is a misnomer since no palm is truly flat. Each palm is curved with mounds of flesh. These elevations are called mounts, and like the rivers of major and minor lines, they can be clues to your personality.

Mounts are found in nine areas of the palm and each has been named after a planet. Traditionally, the traits astrology associates with these planets are also associated with the mounts.

Not all mounts are elevated, though. They may either be flat or built up with flesh. A mount that is elevated indicates a lot of activity in that particular area. The flesh builds up to protect the active blood vessels and nerves in the hand. A mount that is elevated is interpreted to suggest much activity in the areas that it represents. Similarly, if the mount is flat, it is thought to suggest that there is less activity in the area associated with that mount.

When estimating the size and importance of a mount, you always estimate in relation to other mounts on the same hand. First, find the largest mounts on each hand. These are your most important mounts. The attributes associated with those planets will have particular significance for you. But, they are not the *only* mounts which will affect you. Determine your next "major" mount by finding the second largest mounds of flesh on each hand. The characteristics associated with these mounds may also exert a great influence.

It should be remembered that flat mounts are not necessarily negative. For example, most people have elevated mounts below the three fingers of Jupiter, Apollo and Mercury, but a flat mount below the finger of Saturn. A hollow Saturn mount is generally considered a positive sign. It suggests a lightheartedness and an ability to view life with humor. Likewise, a rising

Saturn mount suggests that the person may take life too seriously and can become melancholy.

The true center of the mounts can most accurately be found by taking a palm print. For the purposes of this chapter, it will be enough just to locate your elevated and flat mounts and interpret them. But, in the next chapter, you will learn how to make a palm print and locate the triads, or triangular patterns, on each mount. The triad is considered the true center of the mount and its position represents the extent of influence the mount will have over the personality.

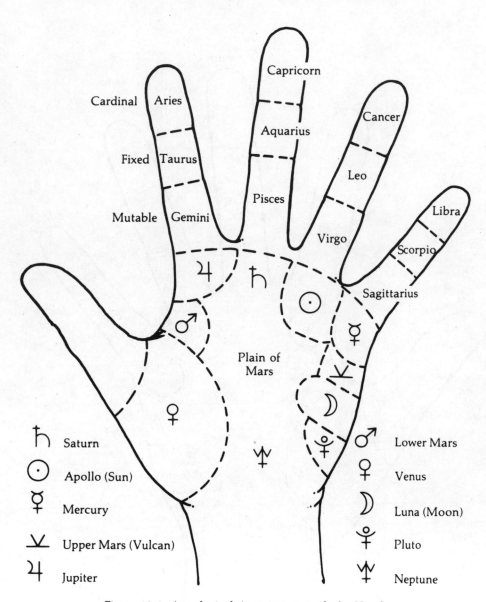

Figure 12-1. Astrological Associations with the Hand

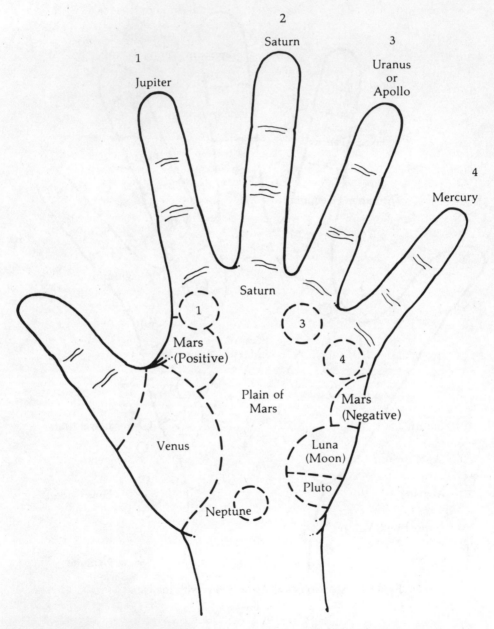

Figure 12-2. Astrological Associations with the Mounts

The Mount of Jupiter

The Mount of Jupiter lies at the base of the index finger. It is the area that contains one's feelings of individuality, strength of character and ego structure. Individualism is the keynote of a strong Jupiter mount. The ambition to be an individual, standing out from the crowd, is indicated by a high mount. Leadership is shown by a strong mount, and the ability to teach others is often present.

A strong mount, combined with a long and sturdy index finger, shows a person who is ambitious to succeed as an individual rather than in a social or professional role. Often success as both is achieved by the strong Jupiterian. But success in a career is always marked by the individualistic approach to work. If the Jupiter finger and mount are overpowered by the Saturn (social roles) mount and finger, the individual will seek titles rather than personal reknown. When the strong Jupiter mount is accompanied by a strong Apollo mount, a prominent personality is added to the strong character and self-will of Jupiter.

The Mount of Self-Reliance

Padding that is built up on the ulnar (non-thumb) side of the hand indicates a desire to take care of one's own needs and be self-sufficient. The activity reflected in this mount is often very great, and sometimes reflects a desire to take care of oneself and others. Now, with the increased emphasis on women to become more independent, this mount is frequently found in women as well as in men.

Mount of Saturn

This mount, found directly below the Saturn finger, is most commonly hollow, rather than elevated. Sometimes it is found between the second and third fingers. Its influence can be evaluated by determining the length of the Saturn finger and the flatness of the mount.

A full Saturn mount directly beneath a long and large middle finger is likely to have the most pure "Saturnian" qualities. The person may be serious, industrious, solitary, cautious and methodical. This type of person is probably a wise investor, since he or she enjoys material goods and has a strong economic sense. A true Saturnian type should guard against becoming too serious.

The opposite extreme is a person with a hollow mount and short Saturn finger (in comparison to the index and third finger). These people can have a very frivolous attitude toward life and may find it difficult to take anything seriously. This finger and mount represent the role we play in society, particularly as it pertains to earthly properties such as real estate. A short Saturn finger and flat mount generally reflect an easy-going attitude toward property matters.

If you find that each hand is different, remember to consider that the left hand reflects your innermost feelings and your right hand indicates your manifest actions in regard to them.

Mount of Apollo

This mount is located under the ring or third finger. The most accurate way to interpret this mount is by considering it in relation to the length of the Apollo finger. If the third finger is large and long (in relation to the other fingers) and the mount is well developed, this person will possess Apollonian characteristics.

He or she is likely to be charming, magnetic, brilliant, warm and colorful. A pure Apollonian type is full of vitality and has a sunny disposition. These qualities make them fine leaders or salespeople. They are also apt to have a strong sense of beauty, drama, intuition and fine taste. If the aesthetic feeling for drama and expression is developed, fame is a possibility. The Apollo finger is also called the "finger of fame." Success of an Apollonian type will be achieved because others are attracted by their magnetism and take notice of them.

The Apollo mount is also called the "happy mount" or the Mount of the Sun. The Appollonian types will pursue occupations that give them personal satisfaction and pleasure first, monetary rewards and recognition second. Their love for the arts is their raison d'etre. They are the people who are artists for their devotion to art, actors because of their pleasure in role-playing, and sculptors for their satisfaction in creation.

If a line extends from the wrist to the Apollo finger, this further reinforces the qualities of Apollo. This person can make a career of the vocation they love. There is some possibility, however, that these capacities can be carried to extremes. If they are developed to excess, the person may become pompous and pretentious. If they are successful, the resultant fame or wealth may upset their emotional stability.

Not everyone has a large mount, long finger, and a line to the Apollo finger, though. Therefore, the degree of influence is reflected by the finger length, mount size, and presence or lack of minor lines in relation to each other. For example, a person with an average finger length and mount, without a line of Apollo, probably has a love for beauty and refinement, but may not pursue an artistic career. They, too, will most likely have a pleasant nature and bright disposition.

Mount of Mercury

This mount is under the little finger. If the little finger is long (in relation to the other fingers), the qualities associated with an elevated mount will be reinforced. Those who are strongly Mercurian types will possess remarkable mental agility. They are cunning and quick thinkers. Their sharp minds often make them eloquent speakers. They are likely to have a talent for commerce and intelligence, and for industry as well. This person may be physically agile. All of these qualities give the Mercurian type great versatility and ingenuity.

If the knuckles of the little fingers are knotted, a discriminating nature is indicated. A knot on the top phalange represents a tendency to use words with precision. Likewise, if the fingers are smooth, the person communicates with a spark of spontaneity. This person has an astute, inventive mind, and a lively wit. These individuals work hard and play hard, since they enjoy using their minds to the maximum.

If the mounts are developed to excess, the person could become materialistic. If the small finger is curved, there is some possibility that the person may use his or her talents dishonestly, becoming an unscrupulous person.

A flat mount may represent lack of activity—mentally and physically. With a little effort, this person can dramatically sharpen his or her mental and physical skills.

Mount of Luna

Look toward the base of the ulna side of the hand, just below the Pluto mount and you will find the location of the Mount of Luna. A highly developed Mount of Luna indicates a person with great powers of creativity and imagination. They are people with poetic and meditative spirits. This mount is often associated with psychic or mystical skills. If the mount is very large, these qualities can be carried to extremes, and there is a danger that the person may become withdawn. When the Mount of Luna is high and firm, it shows a fertile, powerful imagination and a sensitive nature. Likewise, if the mount is high, but soft, this person may need more perseverance to follow through on his or her dreams.

An average mount reflects a sensitive, perceptive, imaginative person who has a strong romantic side. This person likes the water, enjoys travel and admires poetry, art and literature.

A flat mount may represent a person who could use more spontaneity in daily living. These people usually follow a day-to-day routine. They could benefit from a diversion from their daily pattern.

Mount of Lower Mars

The area between the life line and the Mount of Jupiter is the Mount of Lower Mars. In the right hand, it is considered the mount of physical courage; in the left hand, it is associated with emotional courage.

A strong Mount of Lower Mars must be high, full and deeply colored. If the head line is joined to the life line, the qualities associated with this mount will be stronger. This is reinforced further if the head line originates below the life line and within the Lower Mars mount.

A person with a well-developed Lower Mars mount will possess great strength and tenacity. This person has a wonderful competitive spirit and courageous nature. These individuals are aggressive and, as such, make fine leaders. They can be tempestuous, and are sometimes prone to anger. If the lower mount is excessively high (in relation to the other mounts), the person's natural aggression may get out of hand, making them prone to being quarrelsome or, in extreme cases, violent.

Those with a normal mount are usually resolute, courageous and self-controlled. They generally possess a power of resistance.

A flat Lower Mars mount usually reflects a pacifist attitude. These individuals may avoid competition because they do not like aggressive behavior. As a result, they may appear cowardly, but, actually, these people abhor violence.

Mount of Upper Mars

This mount is found above the Luna mount, approximately in the middle of the palm between the head line and the heart line. Like the Mount of Lower Mars, this mount represents the qualities of courage and perseverance. Those with a highly developed mount will be brave and devoted to duty. Morality is important to these people; in addition, they may enjoy detail and admire craftmanship. In excess, there is a possibility for sarcasm and even a bad temper.

A mount that is of average size in comparison to the other mounts will possess these qualities to an average degree. Those with a flat mount are usually not combative types. Their more timid nature can sometimes interfere with them pursuing what they want.

Mount of Venus

The third phalange of the thumb, or the area encircled by the life line, is called the Mount of Venus. The "soft" qualities associated with the Mount of Venus include lovableness, tenderness, and sensuality. This mount represents love of the physical world.

Those with a highly developed, deeply colored and fleshy Venusian mount are very likely passionate people. They have a finely developed sense of touch, appreciate luxury and surrender easily to the sensations they experience. Their sense of music and artistic appreciation is keen. Because a full and fleshy Mount of Venus indicates much activity within the life line, it reflects a person with a zest for life and a spring of physical vitality.

A person with a flat Mount of Venus may indicate a preference to use the mind rather than the body to attain satisfaction for basic needs.

A normal hollowing out of this mount may occur at about age fifty. The "fifty-year hollow" indicates a natural loss of youthful vitality as the body begins to slow down. If it is found in a younger person, it may indicate an unusual loss of physical strength and resistance. This person should rest and eat well, taking precautions not to overextend him- or herself. A period of recuperation will often flesh out this area and decrease the person's susceptibility to illness.

Mount of Neptune

This mount is the area shaped like a triangle in the middle of the base of the palm. In the center of this area, you may find a small bump. Although this is an uncommon elevation, some people do have a developed Mount of Neptune. This reflects a sense of spirituality, mysticism, extra-sensory perception and psychic power. A person with a highly developed Mount of Neptune will have a keen ability to help others by channeling into spiritual forces. This person has dramatic psychic talent and the ability to communicate on the extra-sensory level.

Mount of Pluto

A highly developed Mount of Pluto is a rarity. Found at the very base of the ulna side of the palm, it must bulge upward and outward in order to be considered a truly developed mount. The qualities of mystery and secrecy are associated with a highly developed Plutonian mount. This person's love of intrigue is so strong, he or she could become involved with spying. This individual could also tap into great wells of inner resources indicating a capacity for imagination and sexual fantasy.

Warts, Scars and Markings

Many people consider warts or scars on their hands a blemish to their beauty, but these marks may really be evidence of more than that. A wart or scar can act as a reminder of some emotional conflict—the result of inner fear or pain that was not allowed expression. But, it is the blemish and its placement on the hand that will provide a clue to its origin.

Warts

Warts are often reflective of an unresolved, unexpressed conflict that has been suppressed consciously and forgotten. In such cases, the wart appears as evidence of thwarted expression and will remain until the problem is resolved or disappears.

An illustration of this is a true story of a young married man who had a small wart on the middle section of his right hand on the fourth finger. The small finger is considered the ruler of marriage and all intimate relationships; the middle phalange reflects the realm of the mind. I interpreted the wart as evidence of an unexpressed thought that was in opposition to his wife's thinking. I told him I thought he was in disagreement with his wife about something, but had not told her his feelings. I said it seemed to be an important issue, since its suppression had caused a wart to grow. His wife spoke up immediately and said, "Why didn't you tell me you would really rather move to California instead of Vermont, where I want to go?" He agreed, confessing a strong desire to go to California rather than Vermont.

Scars

A scar on the hands can be interpreted in a similar manner. It is important to consider where the scar appears, as well as whether the wound was self-inflicted or caused by another. Also, check to see the severity of the wound. If the scar is found on the right hand, it represents a wound to the ego and objective life. If it is found in the left hand, it reflects injury to the emotional inner self.

I believe there is no such thing as an accident. All bodily movements are either voluntary or involuntary. As such, scarring can be interpreted as a sign of self-punishment. At some time or another, we all experience feelings which our conscience considers unacceptable. If we do not resolve our guilt feelings about these unacceptable ideas or emotions, it is quite possible that we punish ourselves "accidentally" by hurting ourselves. Our guilt feelings can also attract punishment from others.

Consider, for example, the story of my friend, John. John was everybody's patsy. He could easily be conned into doing others' work. No one suspected that inwardly he resented the role he so often assumed with others. He was also unaware of this inner conflict and so continued to be victimized by those who took advantage of his helpful nature.

For some time, John had been an easy mark for the unpopular duty of dishwashing at the residence he shared with six others. Every night, John did all the dishes. Since he was generally cheerful, no one suspected that he had any complaints.

One night, however, I saw him raise a large chopping knife high into the air to halve a cob of corn, and instead, he severed the tip of a finger. Quietly, without complaint, he waited until everyone had eaten before he asked for a ride to the hospital—the whole time his hand lay on his lap, wrapped in a handkerchief under the table.

This "accident" accomplished two things. John unconsciously punished himself for resenting the work and he ended his ability to do the dishes for some time (and also the conflict over them). The conclusion to the story is that a dishwasher was purchased!

In a society where people are taught not to get angry, complain or be selfish, there are indeed many feelings that are repressed. This repression, in many instances, is both unnatural and unhealthy. It is the type of conflict that often triggers an act of self-punishment, such as an injury to the hand.

Marks

In addition to scars and warts, there are a variety of other marks that appear on many hands. These provide a pictorial representation of their meaning. For example, the mark of the cross—"X"—is a favorable sign that signifies the merger of two energies. As with scars and warts, a more accurate interpretation is possible by consideration of the placement of the mark.

There are a number of basic mark patterns. The following are included among them:

Figure 12-3. Star

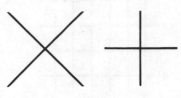

Figure 12-4. Cross

Figure 12-3. This is similar to a tiny round dimple with radiating lines originating from it. It is rarely seen. (This should not be confused with lines intersecting each other.) It depicts good fortune or fame.

Figure 12-4. This is a favorable merger of two energies. An obstacle to be overcome is indicated here.

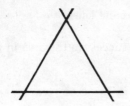

Figure 12-5. Triangle

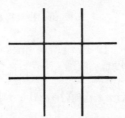

Figure 12-6. Square

Figure 12-5. This shows an obstacle that has to be overcome by two powers that merge. The obstacle is represented as the horizontal line and the two forces are pictured in the second and third sides of the triangle.

Figure 12-6. Two obstacles overcome by two thrusts of energy are suggested in this marking.

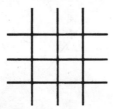

Figure 12-7. Double Square

Figure 12-8. Trident

Figure 12-7. This signifies that three obstacles will be overcome by duplicity of effort.

Figure 12-8. One energy is depicted moving in three directions simultaneously.

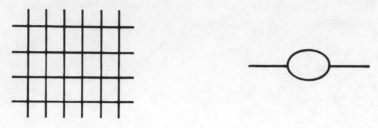

Figure 12-9. Grill   Figure 12-10. Island

Figure 12-9. A complex block to be overcome is depicted here.

Figure 12-10. An island is always found on a line and shows that energy has been divided for a period of time.

Figure 12-11. Small, Short, Horizontal Lines

Figure 12-11. These lines depict barriers to success in the area in which they appear.

Marks on the Mount of Jupiter

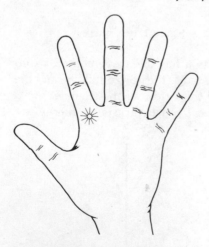

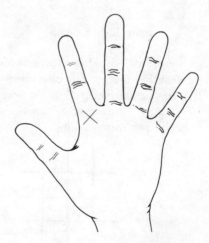

Figure 12-12. Star   Figure 12-13. Cross

Figure 12-12. This marking indicates sudden success or prestige. If it is found only on the left hand, it may mean some difficulty in reaching success. If found only in the right hand, it indicates someone in a position of importance.

Figure 12-13. A happy marriage!

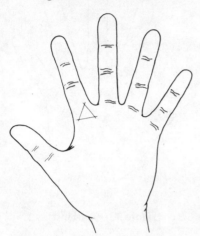

Figure 12-14. Triangle

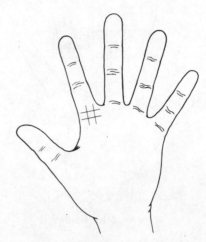

Figure 12-15. Square

Figure 12-14. This is associated with shrewdness, common sense and good management.

Figure 12-15. Teaching ability or a strong sense of self-preservation is evident.

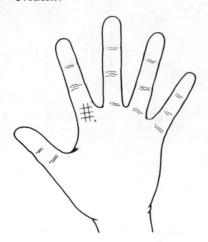

Figure 12-16. Double Square

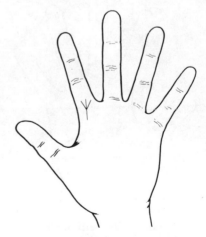

Figure 12-17. Trident

Figure 12-16. This suggests a master teacher.

Figure 12-17. When this mark is found rising from the head line, it signifies a mentally daring and personally courageous individual. A true pioneer!

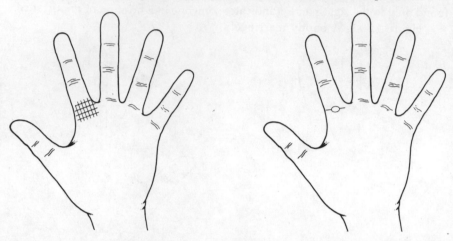

Figure 12-18. Grille   Figure 12-19. Island

Figure 12-18. A grille on the Mount of Jupiter suggests the possibility that the person can become domineering, superstitious or egotistical. The person's pride can become exaggerated.

Figure 12-19. This may depict an unhappy home life, which, if not attended to, could interfere with success.

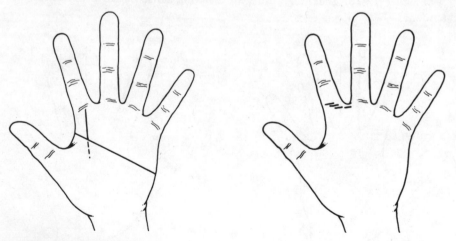

Figure 12-20. Vertical Line   Figure 12-21. Horizontal Lines

Figure 12-20. A vertical line rising from the head line illustrates ambition. If the vertical line crosses the headline, ambition may be thwarted. The person should check to see if any obstacle is interfering with his or her goals.

Figure 12-21. These lines can be blocks to personal success, or perhaps depict a wounded pride. They may also indicate the possibility of bronchial problems.

Marks on the Mount of Saturn

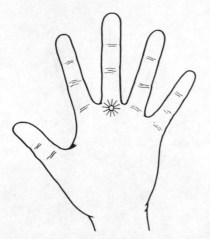

Figure 12-22. Star

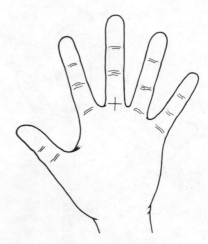

Figure 12-23. Cross

Figure 12-22. This is an ill-fated star. It may suggest a sad or even tragic event. But awareness of problems can stem them.

Figure 12-23. This can signify a person who is accident-prone. Or it may mean that the person needs to spend more time developing their positive qualities.

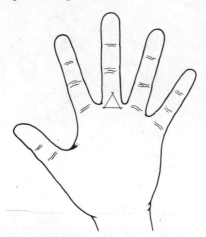

Figure 12-24. Triangle

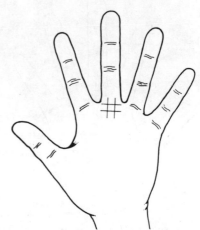

Figure 12-25. Square

Figure 12-24. An ability in the mystic arts is represented here. This person is highly original and would do well in scientific work or other innovative pursuits.

Figure 12-25. This is a protective sign that denotes preservation from disaster or illness.

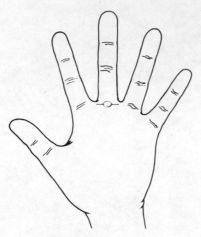

Figure 12-26. Island

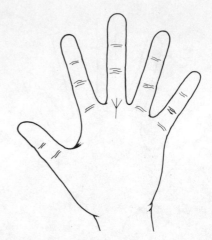

Figure 12-27. Trident

Figure 12-26. Attention may be diverted and increases the possibility of illness or accident. Try to conserve your energy and use it wisely.

Figure 12-27. Material success that will help to secure old age is denoted. This is also a sign of success in philosophical areas.

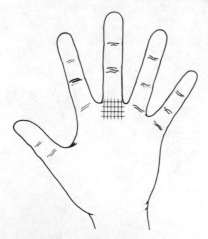

Figure 12-28. Grille

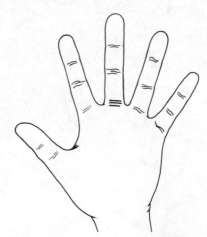

Figure 12-29. Horizontal Lines

Figure 12-28. This sign represents a person whose energies are easily scattered. If prolonged, the dispersion of energy could affect health, particularly circulation and related illnesses such as rheumatism or joint problems. There is also the possibility of hearing difficulties. This person should monitor his or her energy level to bolster disposition and outlook.

Figure 12-29. When these ladder-like lines reach the Jupiter mount, they indicate a climb to accomplishment reached through honest effort. This success is met with outstanding recognition.

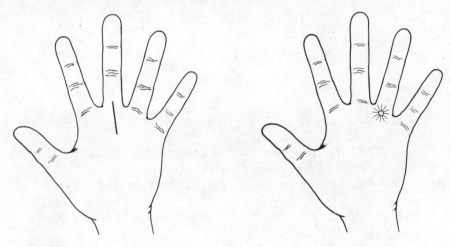

Figure 12-30. Vertical Line   Figure 12-31. Star

Figure 12-30. A single line that runs up and down indicates a single good fortune. If this line is unbroken, it shows a singular solid career that has been uneventful but secure.

Figure 12-31. This star shines with brilliant achievement! However, if the star appears and there is no fate line accompanying it, there may be little satisfaction in the success.

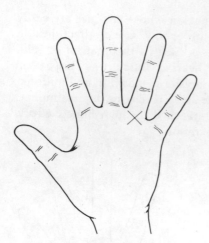

Figure 12-32. Cross

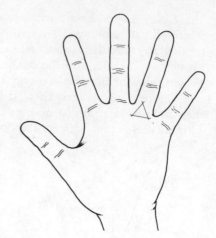

Figure 12-33. Triangle

Figure 12-32. A cross can show that artistic aspirations have met some resistance. However, if the cross is found on top of a fate line to the finger of Apollo, it is likely that the person's creative powers and high ideals will be realized.

Figure 12-33. Artistic ability is cleverly used. As a result, fame and prosperity will likely follow.

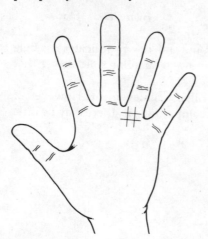

Figure 12-34. Square

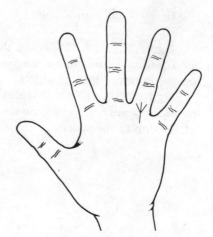

Figure 12-35. Trident

Figure 12-34. This square provides protection against financial loss or loss of reputation.

Figure 12-35. The favors of good luck, fame and fortune are indicated.

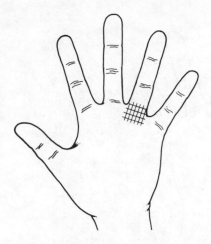

Figure 12-36. Grille

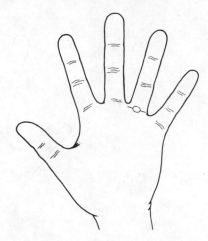

Figure 12-37. Island

Figure 12-36. A performer's personality is denoted. This person enjoys and needs attention, and occasionally is willing to go to great lengths to get it.

Figure 12-37. If energy is divided for extensive periods, it may jeopardize this person's career or hurt their reputation.

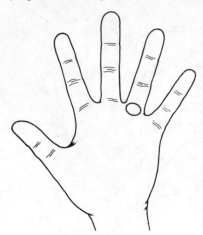

Figure 12-38. Circle

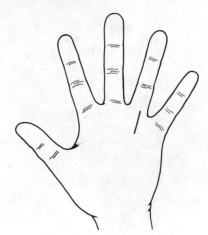

Figure 12-39. Vertical Line

Figure 12-38. This marking shows a person who will most likely enjoy the comforts of fame, glory and success.

Figure 12-39. This is a show of talent and luck. With two lines, the person is gifted with double talents. If many lines are present, there is a danger that the person can scatter his or her energies.

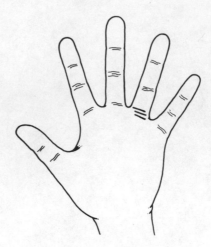

Figure 12-40. Horizontal Lines

Figure 12-40. Talent and success, particularly in literary or commercial areas, are suggested here.

Mount of Mercury

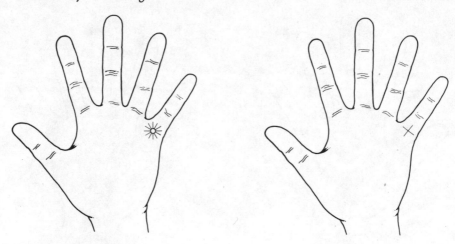

Figure 12-41. Star   Figure 12-42. Cross

Figure 12-41. A star of success! Those with this mark who pursue business, literature, science or public speaking are likely to achieve their aims.

Figure 12-42. This is often found on the hands of writers.

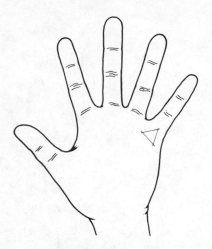

Figure 12-43. Triangle

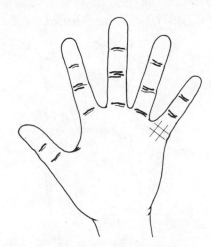

Figure 12-44. Square

Figure 12-43. A penchant for diplomacy and politics is evident.
Figure 12-44. If this person is prone toward restlessness, their meandering nature will be protected.

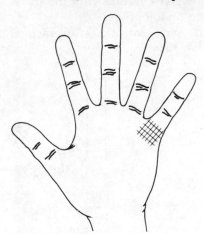

Figure 12-45. Grille

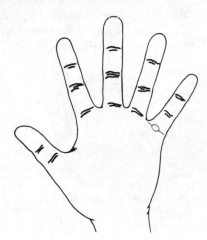

Figure 12-46. Island

Figure 12-45. There is the possibility that energy can be carelessly squandered and the person can become dishonest with him- or herself and others.

Figure 12-46. This person should be careful to use his or her energy to be trustworthy and honest.

Marks on the Mount of Luna

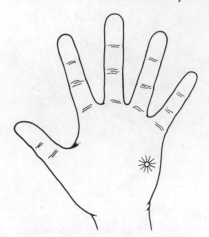

Figure 12-47. Star

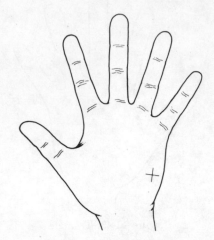

Figure 12-48. Cross

Figure 12-47. This is often found on those prone to sea-sickness or other illnesses connected with water. If the star connects with the travel lines, there is some possibility of a problem on a journey.

Figure 12-48. A very active (and even sometimes overactive) imagination is indicated.

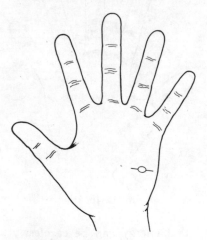

Figure 12-49. Island

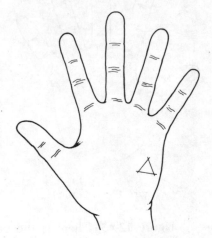

Figure 12-50. Triangle

Figure 12-49. This denotes prophetic dreams and psychic flashes.

Figure 12-50. This person has much more common sense and intuitive ability. Also, a triangle on the Mount of Luna reflects expertise at sailing.

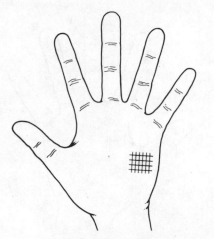

Figure 12-51. Grille

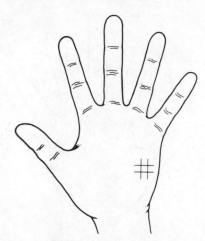

Figure 12-52. Square

Figure 12-51. The dispersion of energy can effect disposition and increase stress and anxiety.

Figure 12-52. This protects the individual while traveling.

Marks on the Mount of Lower Mars

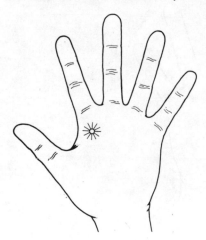

Figure 12-53. Star

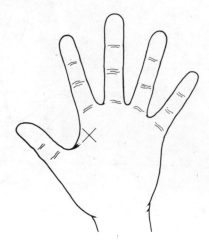

Figure 12-54. Cross

Figure 12-53. This can indicate the loss of someone close or it may be a sign of conflict. This person could be a fine military commander.

Figure 12-54. This person is very hard on him- or herself. They should develop more self-acceptance.

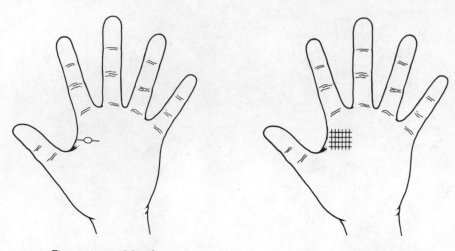

Figure 12-55. Island   Figure 12-56. Grille

Figure 12-55. An island like this reflects the pockets of less happy times, most likely during childhood.

Figure 12-56. This person's aggressive instincts are heightened.

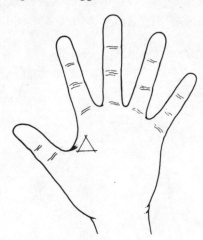

Figure 12-57. Triangle

Figure 12-57. Meritorious courage and enterprise are shown. Military distinction is a possibility.

Marks on the Mount of Upper Mars

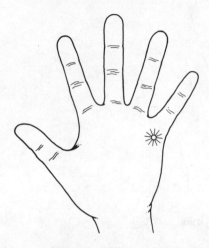

Figure 12-58. Star

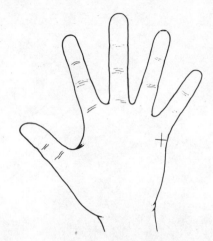

Figure 12-59. Cross

Figure 12-58. This person should pay attention to his or her own health. If this star is accompanied by a line of Apollo, his or her strong character may enable a personal achievement worth noting.

Figure 12-59. Be watchful so that an aggressive instinct doesn't get out of hand and provoke trouble.

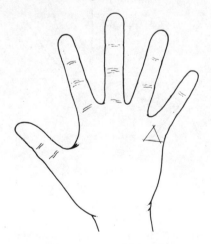

Figure 12-60. Triangle

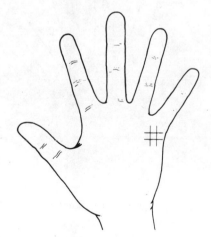

Figure 12-61. Square

Figure 12-60. Military skill is represented.
Figure 12-61. Protection from bodily harm is evident.

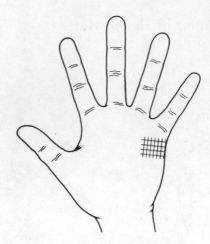

Figure 12-62. Grille

Figure 12-62. This person should take precautions to avoid accidents or violence.

Marks on the Mount of Venus

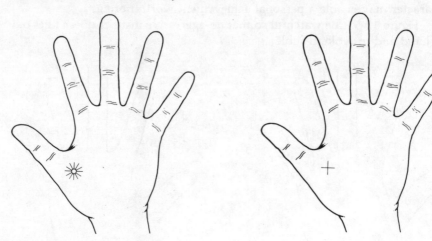

Figure 12-63. Star   Figure 12-64. Cross

Figure 12-63. Lucky in love! Less fortunate if the star is found toward the base of the wrist, though.

Figure 12-64. This may show obstacles encountered, particularly with relatives, if the cross touches the life line.

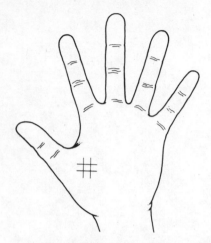

Figure 12-65. Square

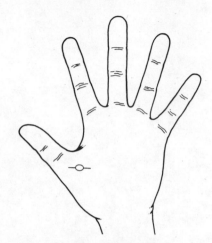

Figure 12-66. Island

Figure 12-65. A strong sense of self-preservation is indicated. If the square is too close to the life line, the person may experience self-protection as confinement, though.

Figure 12-66. This person can divide their energy between several lovers, because of a devotion for the opposite sex.

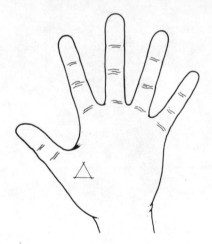

Figure 12-67. Triangle

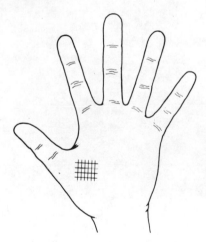

Figure 12-68. Grille

Figure 12-67. This reflects shrewdness in matters of love.

Figure 12-68. The grille represents an affectionate nature and even sexual magnetism.

13

Dermaglyphics

The literal Greek translation of *dermaglyphics* is skin engravings. Like the hieroglyphics, the picture symbols used by the ancient Egyptians, the symbols that form the unique skin patterns of our hands can be read and interpreted, bringing new insights and personal knowledge.

Just as no two snowflakes are alike, no two people have the same patterns on their hands. Each person has a wholly distinctive set of skin markings. Most people understand that since everyone's fingerprints are different, they can be used for identification purposes, but few also realize the markings found throughout the rest of the palm are entirely original, too. Often, these patterns even differ between the two hands of the same individual. These complex patterns of ridges and furrows remain unchanged throughout your life, and are virtually indestructible.

The term *Dermatoglyphics* was coined by Harold Cummins of Tulane in 1926 to describe the study of skin patterns. The knowledge gleaned from research into these patterns has grown since this field began, and it has had much impact in a number of scientific fields.

The derma patterns are formed early in fetal life. During the twelfth week of gestation, at which time the fetus begins to show signs of individuality, markings and undulations appear on the inner surface of the epidermal layers. These later become the ridges and furrows that contain the sweat glands.

This pattern never changes. It increases in size as the individual grows, but the pattern remains the same. Fingerprints cannot be destroyed unless a serious injury is done to the deepest layer of the epidermis. It is true that even ancient mummies have clear and identifiable prints.

If you compare the prints of any two people, innumerable differences on the fingers and palms can be observed. This is true even with sets of identical twins. With them, the general outline may be similar, but the detail of the patterns will vary.

Fingerprints were first used in police work after Sir Francis Galton noted in the late 1800s that fingerprints were an ideal means of identification. But, using fingerprints as a form of identification does not have to be limited to police work. An interesting sequence in the movie *The Andromeda Strain* showed a computer scanning a hand to identify a person for admission to a maximum security lab complex.

Not only can finger and hand prints be used to identify an individual, prints can identify an individual's personal traits, too. That is the focus of the field of Dermatoglyphics. Scientists are deciphering these patterns in order to identify personality and physical traits that are inborn. Many researchers believe that certain types of patterns are associated with certain personality and physical traits.

It should be noted that Dermatoglyphics is *not* the study of the lines of the hands, such as the heart line, head line or life line. It deals strictly with skin patterns such as papillary ridges, which appear on the palm side of the hand, or other patterns with which one is born.

Dermaglyphic Maps

The most accurate way to study the derma patterns is to make a print of the palm side of the hand. This can be used as a map to read the hands' distinctive patterns.

The ink method is similar to that used by police for identification of criminals and also used by hospitals to identify newborns. This is not only easy, but is also an interesting way to obtain an accurate print. Always label the print with the person's name, age, address, sex and any other information you want to include.

To make a print, you will need:

- black, water-base linoleum-block printing ink
- a 4-inch hard rubber roller (called a brayer)
- white, shiny, smooth 8×11 paper
- layers of foam padding or towels

On a tile, flat block of plastic, glass, or even heavy cardboard wrapped with tinfoil, squeeze ⅓ inch of ink. Roll the brayer back and forth in the ink until the roller is evenly coated and beginning to lose its wet shiny look. The object is to get as little ink on the hands as necessary in order to get a print.

Roll the brayer over the palm of the hand from the wrist to the fingertip. Be sure to stretch the fingertips out and cover the entire palm with ink. Next, place a sheet of paper on top of the padding. Grab the wrist and while it is relaxed, press onto the paper. Slide your other hand to the underneath of the padding and apply pressure in order to get a print of the center of the palm. To get a good print of the thumb, it is advisable to roll the thumb on its "face" when pressing the hand onto the paper. Repeat until you have a good clear print of each hand.

The gum camphor method is another method of making a palm print. This is sometimes less messy than working with ink.

To make a print, you will need:

• gum camphor
• white typewriter paper
• a plate
• foam padding or towels as a cushion
• "Fixatif" (optional), which is available at art supply stores

Put a small piece of gum camphor on a plate. Light it with a match and rapidly pass a sheet of typewriter paper over the flame until the paper becomes deep black all over. Be careful not to let the paper become yellow or burn by exposing it to the flame too closely or for too long.

Place the sheet over padding. Place the palm on the prepared sheet, pressing down firmly. Slide the hand underneath the padding and apply pressure so as to get a print of the center of the palm. Then, before lifting the hand, outline the hand using a well-sharpened pencil. Try to avoid smudging the print when lifting the hand. Then, preserve with "Fixatif." Take prints of both hands, repeating until you have satisfactory prints.

Derma Patterns

There are a number of identifiable patterns found in the palms. The placement of these patterns reflects certain traits associated with them. Identifiable patterns include papillary ridges, triads, loops, double loops, whorls, arches and tented arches.

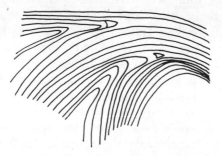

Figure 13-1. Papillary Ridges

Papillary ridges (Figure 13-1) look like swirling hair sweeping across the hand. The ridges run in streams, in groups of three, which occasionally combine to form a triangle or triad. The papillary ridges can be very fine, barely visible to the naked eye or so large as to be quite obvious. Usually, the papillary ridges of men are larger than the finer ridges of women.

In general, the finer the ridges are, the more refined and sensitive the person is. If fine ridges are combined with silky smoothness, it is likely that the person's aesthetic sense is highly developed.

Very large papillary ridges denote an extremely active, physically-oriented person. These people tend to have a higher tolerance of pain—both physically and emotionally. They are difficult to hurt and most often excel as athletes or physical laborers. Because they are less sensitive to pain, they are also less likely to be aware of pain in others. This quality makes them sometimes appear to be insensitive.

Figure 13-2. Triads

The triad (Figure 13-2) is a triangle formed by the merging of papillary ridges. Triads are considered places of power. Wherever three lines are joined, it is thought to be a place of your personal power. The more triads found in your hands, the more complex your life will be. This is because you have many more sources of personal power available.

In addition to the triads often found below the fingers, some people have triads on the fingertips. Those without triads on their fingertips are usually the workers of the world. They are the types of people upon whom society depends to carry the work load and maintain the status quo.

A single triad on a fingertip shows that the person could use the help of a mate for fulfillment in that area. If two triads are present, the person can achieve success alone and usually prefers to. Two triads in the fourth finger, the finger of marriage, could be a sign of marital problems.

Everyone has a triad between Venus and Luna. If this triad is found closer to the thumb, it indicates that you will use your energy yourself. If this triad is found closer to the radial side, it shows energy moving outward, usually in service to others.

Any additional triads besides those on the fingertips, below the fingertips, or between Venus and Luna, are extra. They reflect special abilities or talents, which very often have been passed on genetically through generations.

Look at the prints you have made and outline all the triads with a fine red ballpoint pen. Count the triads on each hand, noting the sum at the top of the print. Do both hands have an equal number of triads and therefore an equal distribution of power? If a person has less than four, he or she may be unhealthy, with possible genetic defects. Generally, half of the fingers should have at least one energy point. On the average, most people have ten triads on each hand—five in the palm and one on each finger. A person with exceptional drive is indicated if there are more than ten triads per hand.

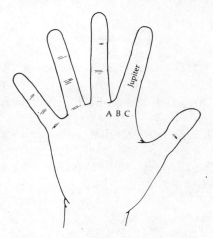

Figure 13-3. Triads Under Jupiter

Figure 13-3A. This person is united with society. He or she identifies with societal roles and depends on others.

Figure 13-3B. This person has much power to achieve self-actualization. He or she is a self-starter and is very self-sufficient.

Figure 13-3C. Because this triad is closer to the thumb, the person feels farther from society (represented in the middle finger) and is more self-willed (represented in the thumb). He or she is likely to be a loner who may have difficulty relating to others.

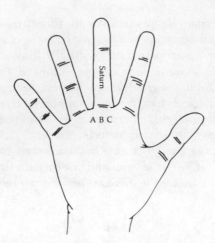

Figure 13-4. Triads Under Saturn

Figure 13-4A. This individual tends to be self-sacrificing, playing out roles to benefit others.

Figure 13-4B. This triad denotes that the self and society are united and both benefit.

Figure 13-4C. This triad represents a tendency to play out roles for self-satisfaction in service to the ego.

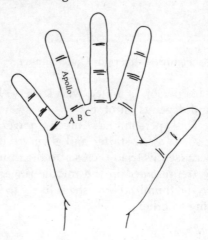

Figure 13-5. Triads Under Apollo

Figure 13-5A. This depicts a person to whom art is expressed as the communication of new ideas.

Figure 13-5B. This denotes a person whose creative art is sparked by relating to other artists.

Figure 13-5C. This person's creative efforts are devoted to society and particularly group welfare systems.

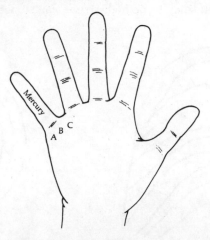

Figure 13-6. Triads Under Mercury

Figure 13-6A. Here, body language is used to influence others.
Figure 13-6B. This person uses self-expression to unite others.
Figure 13-6C. This formation indicates a person for whom body language is the expression of self-actualization, as with the dancer or artist.

Although the triads are considered the seats of power, there are also other patterns that wield their influence. The following are general descriptions of a number of patterns.

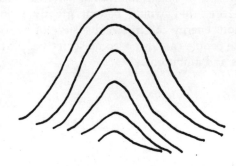

Figure 13-7. Loop   Figure 13-8. Tented Arch

The loop (Figure 13-7) reflects mental and emotional elasticity. A loop generally indicates great flexibility, adaptability and versatility. The reactiveness associated with the loop may also denote a predisposition to digestive, nervous or heart problems.

Figure 13-8 reflects a highly sensitive, and particularly artistic or musical temperament. This skin formation can denote impulsivity and reactiveness. The tendency to be high-strung can sometimes be linked with nervous disorders.

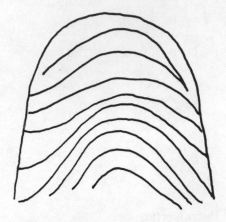

Figure 13-9. Arch   Figure 13-10. Whorl

This skin formation (Figure 13-9) is linked with a tendency to repress feelings and ideas. Such a pattern may show difficulty in expressing thoughts and feelings. This may be interpreted by others as a reserved nature. The person with arches is less impulsive and less likely to carefully weigh each decision. Their repressive tendencies may manifest themselves as ulcers or other digestive weaknesses.

Figure 13-10 is a sign of an individual who will probably have significant personal ambitions. Their ambitions can create inner tension; therefore, they would benefit greatly from additional relaxation. This nervous energy can trigger digestive or heart problems if it is not checked. These people can also become secretive, particularly about their individual ideas and ambitions.

Figure 13-11. Composite Loops

The formation in Figure 13-11 shows the ability to see both sides of an argument. While this complex loop is usually found among very intelligent people, it may also be the mark of those who have a hard time making a decision, precisely because they can see both sides of a matter.

Other Derma Patterns

Do you have any of the following patterns? These patterns are found in specific places in the palms and denote special characteristics. Can you find any in your hands?

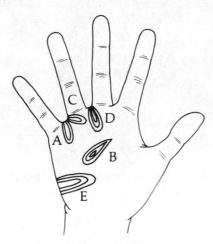

Figure 13-12. Loop Patterns

Figure 13-12A shows the ability to enjoy laughter and get a great deal of pleasure from the humor found in life. These individuals are able to see the lighter sides of living and most likely enjoy life immensely.

Figure 13-12B denotes a very keen memory. This pattern can also be an encouraging sign for those who want to develop their psychic awareness, particularly in the realm of the memory of the universe, called the akashic records.

Figure 13-12C denotes great pride and self-confidence. Personal ease and social grace make dealing with the public a natural for those with this pattern.

Figure 13-12D represents the ability to work hard at goals. Those with this mark take their work seriously. They are intent and intense and also possess remarkable common sense.

Figure 13-12E. This person is keenly attuned to nature and this is an extra dimension of their psychic self. They perceive all plant and animal life with understanding and are even aware of water, minerals, and other natural resources that share the planet. They are happiest in natural settings, where they sense the strong rhythms of life and nature.

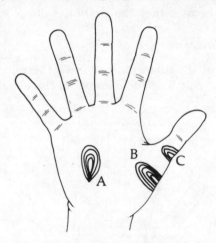

Figure 13-13. Loop Patterns

Figure 13-13A. This pattern shows the capacity for inspiration. This person is both inspired and can inspire others. Their idealism spurs that quality in others.

Figure 13-13B reflects strong rapport with life. These people respond quickly to their environment. They react to moods—the moods of music, of others, or even of nature. Because of this sensitivity to their surroundings, their emotions fluctuate wildly. They will need to develop more self-control to handle this tendency.

Those individuals with a loop pattern such as the one in Figure 13-13C, have a natural sense of rhythm. They have a great love of melody and harmony. They may have an aptitude in music or potential dancing skills.

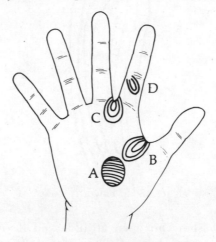

Figure 13-14. Loop Patterns

Figure 13-14A is called the "beehive" because it resembles the striped back of a bee. It denotes musical genius in one form or another. It possibly reflects an aptitude as a composer, or certainly a musician.

Figure 13-14B represents natural strength and generally indicates a person with great character and courage. This loop shows endurance, stamina and fearlessness.

Figure 13-14C is known as the "Rajah Loop" since it was first found in India on the palms of royal descendants. It is now taken to denote great dignity and very often leadership qualities. Especially, if the finger of Jupiter is prominent, it is likely to be found on the hand of a true leader.

Figure 13-14D reflects great charisma. These people seem to exert great power over others. They can be magnetic and hypnotic.

Derma Patterns Found on the Fingers

The study of Dermatoglyphics also includes interest in the types of patterns found on the tips of fingers, commonly called fingerprints. In addition to serving as a form of identification, fingerprints can "identify" certain tendencies in individuals and particular characteristics that are likely.

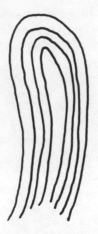

Figure 13-15. Fingertip Loops

Loops generally show an open attitude and flexible nature. When found on the fingers, the loop influences the traits represented in that particular finger. If you have loops on all your fingers and thumbs, you are probably very broad-minded. It is likely that you are interested in many things, are open to suggestion, and are easy to get along with. You are probably a good team player since you are cooperative and work well in groups. Your flexibility increases your ability to cope with the uncertainties of life. You adjust well to the demands of any situation you encounter.

However, you can suffer from your widespread interests—you may find you can divide and scatter your energies in too many places at once. Not only can this be tiring, you may also accomplish less than if you pursued fewer interests. You are also easygoing and this, too, may hamper your achievements unless you are otherwise encouraged.

If you find loops on both little fingers, you will probably prefer a "team approach" in your close relationships, and particularly, in marriage. You are flexible within your relationships and are happiest when the other person is also flexible. You are open to other people and are broad-minded. A close relationship for you will be a way to expand your life experience. You eagerly welcome the opportunity to learn and grow within your intimate relationships.

Loops on both ring fingers are a sign that you have great tolerance for the foibles of friends and society. You are also open-minded in your attitude toward the arts and make a pleasant, amiable companion. The loops indicate your capacity to expand your awareness of drama, music and art, developing a discriminating and fine artistic taste.

If you have loops on both middle fingers, it represents your ability to get along with many types of people and cooperate in any venture. Since you work well in a group or on a team, you are a valuable employee. This trait gives you a wide spectrum of careers to choose from. Since so many pursuits attract you, you may try more than one! At home, you also advocate a team approach, encouraging your family to work together to improve the situation at home.

Index fingers with loops represent your attitude toward power and authority, showing a belief in achievement through cooperation. Your flexibility makes you amenable to suggestions and change. All of this increases your ability to make decisions. Since you are generally eager to improve your personality, you will undergo much inner growth and development.

If you have loops on both thumbs, you are probably willing to cooperate and learn from others in order to achieve your goals. Since the loops represent flexibility, you may find you have difficulty enforcing your will, represented in the thumbs. Instead, you may find it easier to go along with a stronger-willed individual, since you so strongly desire harmonious relationships and conditions.

Clockwise   Concentric   Counterclockwise

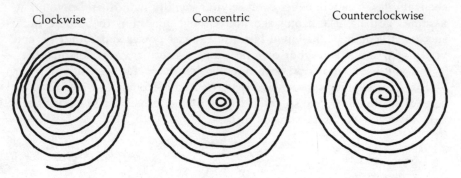

Figure 13-16. Whorls

Usually whorls represent an individualized style, a unique quality and a strong belief system. Depending on which finger the whorl is located, it will represent various unique qualities and beliefs that make the person stand apart from the rest.

If you have whorls on all your fingers and thumbs, you are truly exceptional! This is a rare configuration and represents a very unusual person. Tremendous energy is available for you to use toward your many pursuits. You may be somewhat fixed with decided tastes, likes and dislikes. You tend to spend time with those who think as you do. You have a strong will to enforce your ideas and the ability to prove their credibility. You have all the resources and power to overcome any obstacles you might encounter. Others will perceive your drive, strength, and your unique character, and admire you.

If you have whorls on your little fingers, it indicates you are idealistic and have definite expectations of close relationships. You will brook no interference in achieving your standards for marriage. Therefore, you will be happiest if you find a spouse with similar ideas and values.

Whorls on both ring fingers show that because you know what you like, you are not easily influenced in your choice of friends, music, or art. You can also make a career of a creative talent in music, art, poetry or drama. You will most likely have a need for self-expression, so pursuing an artistic career will be satisfying. Generally, you are very creative and have an interesting personality.

If you have whorls on both middle fingers, your family, home and career will be very important to you. You will expend much energy in these areas and your experience there will never be ordinary. The areas of family, home and career will be avenues for you to express your own unique talents.

When there are whorls on both index fingers, you will have quite an interesting personality and individualistic lifestyle. You are more concerned with unraveling the mystery of your self-identity than pursuing traditional societal roles. You will never confuse your identity with the roles you may assume. You have a strong ego and enough ambition to become quite successful. You have the latent talent to exercise power and authority, and you prefer to make all your own decisions concerning your personal life.

If you have whorls on both thumbs, you have a powerful will. Your will to live, express and achieve is particularly strong. You like to be in control of situations, and so you prefer to be the "boss." These whorls are a very favorable configuration for success.

Figure 13-17. Tented Arches

The tented arch (Figure 13-17) is the symbol of the mountain climber, the one who strives to achieve and who labors to climb higher. People with tented arches know where they want to go and realize they will only arrive at their goals through their own efforts. Ambitious and active, they are willing to do everything themselves in order to satisfy their yearnings.

Because they have set their sights on foreseeable goals, they often look to the future, not only for themselves, but also for others. You are apt to find people with tented arches striving for the common good, for any progressive movement attracts them. They are often interested in social reforms or political causes and prefer careers which provide avenues for such involvements. Progressive education, innovative therapies, the latest ideas all interest them.

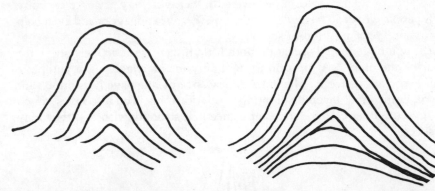

Figure 13-18. Tented Arch Without Triad

Figure 13-19. Tented Arch with Triad

Figure 13-18 represents a "plugger" who tries to get others to join in to reform the status quo. These people are practical, reliable and very industrious. Their independent nature bucks when they are bossed around, since they tend to be stubborn.

Because the triad (Figure 13-19) is the seat of power, those with a triad have desires similar to those without, but have much more concentrated power to reinforce their efforts. It is almost as if a hidden power fueled their upward mobility. These people possess remarkable determination and if opposed, they can become fiercely aggressive.

If you have tented arches on both thumbs, it is likely that you have a strong ambition to succeed in life. You are very active, particularly in your efforts to improve conditions. Your interest in the future increases your desire to witness new frontiers. You move gracefully forward into the future, leaving the past behind you as you change the present. Your generosity is notable since you are more interested in seeing improvements for all, rather than your own.

When both middle fingers have tented arches, it suggests strong personal ambition. Upwardly mobile, you leave old friends behind as you meet your goals. Your interest in self-improvement will reign supreme.

If the middle fingers—which represent the area of job, career, home and family—have tented arches, you will be interested in continually improving each of those realms. Vocations that attract you will have to be quick-paced and constantly changing, especially if they offer avenues to make changes within society. You will be open to the latest ideas about home improvement and family living, as well. Alternative lifestyles will appeal to you, as will innovative theories of education and learning.

Ring fingers with tented arches, which reflect your social life and self-expression, suggest a strong emphasis on friends with similar interests. Your interest in *avant garde* drama and art will introduce you to many who share your enthusiasm. You are socially active and have particular admiration for those you consider to be over-achievers. In fact, you may prefer to socialize with people who you feel will support you in your endeavors and even help to advance your position in society.

If you have tented arches on both little fingers, you actively strive for security and status. A top priority will be your marriage, since you have high expectations for it. The outer appearance of marriage is as important to you as the inner meaning of intimate relationships. You also invest much energy into other close relationships since you strongly wish that they may be successful.

Figure 13-20. Double Loops

Double loops (Figure 13-20) are symbolic of good judgment. Those with double loops weigh their decisions carefully, and avoid hasty or impulsive behavior.

Two thumbs with double loops suggest wise judgment, particularly when deciding upon goals. Thumbs reflect a person's willpower in reaching goals. You require all the facts before making an assessment and avoid haste or impulsivity when setting goals. You are quite capable of making evaluations. Like a judge who carefully considers all the evidence, you also thoroughly deliberate before reaching a decision. However, it may appear to others that you are deliberately slow to make decisions. With such careful consideration, you possess fine judgment, particularly when defining goals and the best ways to achieve them.

Two index fingers with double loops show the ability to be an excellent judge of others. One of your strongest traits is your capacity to accurately judge yourself and others. You are unlikely to reach your decisions before all the facts are in. Because of this, you may have difficulty determining the best route for your personal ambitions since the roads are endless and it is nearly impossible to consider them all. Generally, you are very fair when in a position of authority. Your judgments are just because you take the time to consider all points of view.

If you have a double loop on your right middle finger, you will very likely excel in any career in which you are called upon to make decisions. Your impartial evaluations and your ability to perceive all facets of any problem render you particularly competent in a position of decision-making. Your decisions are logical and based on fact, never on emotions.

Likewise, double loops on the left hand indicate that your instinctive judgment is outstanding. Your subconscious mind works like a computer, assembling all the facts and releasing a decision in the form of a hunch or an idea.

14

Hands and Your Health

Hands hold many clues to our physical, emotional and mental conditions; their appearance, color, flexibility and state of tension or relaxation provide bits of information to interpret our overall condition. Hands show stress in any number of ways and this is often evidence of other health problems or concerns.

Flexibility

Some physical culturists believe that flexibility—not strength or endurance—is the most important physical trait. They believe that as we age, our tendons shorten and our bodies lose mobility and adaptability. However, if we are limber and flexible, our bodies will age gracefully.

Hands reflect that philosophy in miniature. How flexible are you? Can you bend with a storm in your environment or do you stiffen to resist the elements?

Test your hand flexibility by following this experiment. Press one hand down on the other with the palms touching. See how much resistance the bottom hand has when you press down on it. Now, try to press back the fingers to see how far back they will go. Do the same thing with the thumbs. Are they stiff and rigid, or flexible and pliant?

The degree of flexibility generally shows the state of emotional and mental health and elasticity. Flexibility suggests both physical agility and an agile, intuitive mind. It further suggests an ability to adjust to the demands of the environment. Emotionally, those with limber hands adapt well to their environment, since they can cope with various changes, stresses, and pressures. In contrast, very stiff fingers indicate a tense person who has a stiff and rigid outlook on life.

If the tips of the fingers are more flexible than the rest of the finger, versatility is noted. However, if the tips are bent back even in a normal resting position, the person probably goes through money very quickly, since it figuratively rolls right out of their hands.

Color

The hand is a particularly rich source of information for a doctor familiar with the health language of the hands. Changes of color have particular significance in evaluating health.

• An abnormal yellow color may indicate cardiovascular problems. This is due to the presence of blood fats such as cholesterol and triglycerides. If hands appear yellow, blood tests should be done as a precautionary measure.
• Pale palms may be evidence of low blood pressure.
• A pronounced reddening of the palms is called palmar erythmea and is quite normal in pregnant women, but otherwise may suggest cirrhosis of the liver. Doctors quite aptly call these palms "liver palms." Very red palms may also suggest hypertension.
• If your hands become bronze or brownish looking, have your liver checked.

Fingernails

Changes in fingernails can also represent health concerns. Do not try to treat yourself if you find any of the following nail conditions. Go to a competent diagnostician.

• Brittle or thickened nails could show the possibility of cardiovascular diseases, or disorders of the endocrine system, such as hormonal, thyroid or pituitary deficiencies.
• A slate gray or blue-black nail can be evidence of silver or lead poisoning. Green nails may indicate chronic exposure to chrome, while blue nails may mean there has been an exposure to cobalt.
• A totally white nail can be a sign of liver disease. A half-red and half-white nail may show symptoms of kidney disease.

Skin Texture and Temperature

As was discussed earlier in the book, the texture and temperature of the skin can reflect certain physical and emotional conditions. Do any of these apply to you?

• Dry skin may show a nutritional deficiency. The skin condition is evidence that the person is not satisfying total dietary needs.

• A slightly moist, thin-skinned hand can indicate the beginnings of rheumatoid arthritis.

• If you are a smoker and your fingers are usually icy cold, your smoking may be constricting blood vessels in the extremities and damaging your body. Under normal conditions, your hands should be comfortably warm.

• If sweating causes eczema on your palms, it may indicate an ulcer.

Lines and Dermaglyphs

Variations of lines or derma patterns may suggest abnormalities in physical health, or the presence of disease. Or, they may simply suggest the need for rest and an improved diet.

• A chained line can be evidence of a lack of potassium.

• Pale lines may show the need for iron. This condition can also be interpreted to represent a lack of sleep or nourishment.

• Fading lines found in the palm suggest a copper deficiency. This decreases elasticity and flexibility.

Hands in Repose and Action

The state of the muscles in the hands represents the inner state of the individual. The constant motion of the muscles, both tiny involuntary muscles and the large voluntary muscles, speak their own language about the physical condition.

Watch the hands of others as they pass through their routine of the day—walking, talking, sitting. You will see a well-adjusted individual walk along, arms swinging gently, hands relaxed and palms partially open. Likewise, a cautious, self-contained individual has little swinging in the arms and the fingers are usually firmly closed. Their physical stance reflects their emotional attitude—a serious, firm and determined person.

If you see one whose fingers are nearly open, hands limp and lifeless, dangling with no swinging motion, it is likely you are watching the walk of someone who lacks purpose and who is indecisive and suggestible. The opposite of this type is a person whose arms, hands and fists are closed firmly, showing promising determination.

Do you want to know vital energetic people? Look for those with springy, elastic hands and arms. Like body langauge, the hands express their own messages.

Here are some examples of typical hand and arm motions and their meanings:

• If the right hand and arm are held vertically and the left has a slight bend at the elbow, this person is dominated by artistic qualities, love of refinement and culture, and perhaps some psychic ability.

• If the right hand is vertical, loose and drooping, and the left hand is drooping at the wrist, it is likely the person is hypersensitive and can be finicky.

• If both hands move constantly, the person is probably under a great deal of stress due to the changing emotions he or she is undergoing.

• Someone who holds their hands in front or on the side, waving them about like antennas to keep from touching anything, is probably sizing everything up and avoids contact. These individuals travel through life alert and watchful.

• If a person constantly toys with an object, it denotes nervousness or excitement.

• When hands are clasped easily together in front, palm side up, it shows calm and repose. This person has an even temper and is slow, unruffled and dignified. However, if the fists are clenched and elbows bent, it suggests a bullying nature. Clenched fists indicate suppressed anger.

• A private person often walks with hands clasped in back. They like to keep their thoughts to themselves and prefer not to expose their feelings. Hiding your hands behind your back indicates extreme caution and sometimes suspicion of others.

• Biting nails may be evidence that the person is unable to express anger or hostility, and instead turns it inward. Licking fingers may symbolize a person who is still "licking wounds" received earlier in life. Rubbing hands together can reflect nervous anxiety or a tendency to fabricate.

• Arms and hands swinging in rhythm with the walk is a natural motion, especially for those at ease with themselves and the world they live in. They are comfortable, vital and open to new experiences.

• When the hands are steepled, fingers touching each other and pointing upward, it is probable that the person is confident of their own authority. One often sees this steepling during interviews of authorities or speakers. Another stance of authority is when the person rests the hands on either hip.

Exercises for Healthy Hands

To keep your hands limber, your joints flexible and circulation moving, there are a number of simple exercises that can help. Hand exercises should become a part of your daily routine and as you become more conscious of your hands you will also become more aware of what your hands tell you. The principle is simple—take care of your hands and they will take care of you.

Wrist Mobility

Sit down on a chair and hold your arms straight out in front of you. Shake your hands up and down loosely. This helps the mobility of the wrist, increases circulation and reduces the chance of cramps.

Hand Stretch

Hold both hands up in front of your face and make fists. Then spread your fingers outward and upward, stretching them as far as you can. Do this as many times as you comfortably can.

Finger Stretch

Hold your hands up in front of you, palms facing you, about a foot from your face. Very slowly, fold your thumbs across the inside of the palms, without moving any other fingers, and then slowly return to the starting position. Repeat several times. Then, one at a time, bring all your fingers down toward your wrist and back into place.

The Clasp

Clasp your hands together with the fingers interlaced and thumbs on top. Wiggle the thumbs vigorously. Do the same with each finger, one at a time.

Finger Massage

With one hand, grasp the digits of the other hand, one at a time, at the base. Massage toward the tip with a rotating motion, like a corkscrew, stretching each digit gently as you massage outward.

Pencil Press

With a pencil, press gently into the groove between each finger. Up and down, press as firmly as is comfortable. This releases energy that may be locked up. If there is a sharp pain, do it slowly until the pain disappears. If there is a dull ache, use a massaging motion, or replace the pencil with your hand and squeeze and massage that area until the ache is gone. Do this to each hand.

Hand Massage

With one hand, clasp the other around the wrist firmly. With a slight stretching movement and twisting as you go, massage the whole hand, ending at the fingertips. Close your eyes and imagine energy filling your hands. Focus your attention on your hands and continue until they tingle. Imagine tension leaving through the fingertips, and then imagine energy coming into your hands through the center of the palms. Now, focus on your left hand and imagine it being filled with a beautiful, glowing pink energy. Next, visualize the right hand being filled with a beautiful sky-blue vital force that calms and tranquilizes it. Enjoy the relaxation for a few moments.

15

Vocational Hand Analysis

Like a doctor who collects information by conducting a number of interviews, examinations and tests, before making a prognosis, so you are now able to review your own assessments of the lines, marks, derma patterns, color, texture and shape of the hands, and make an overall evaluation.

Throughout this book, you have learned how to examine the hands. You have discovered how the shape, marks, lines and colors of the hands relate to each other and to each individual's emotional climate. This holistic approach has helped you to learn about the physical state of your hands as it relates to your emotional and physical well-being.

Throughout the book, I have discussed a number of factors including the relationship between the right and left hands and the opposite hemispheres of the brain; hand color, texture, and size; hand dominance; finger and phalange length; nail types; thumb significance; hand mounts; the major and minor palmar lines; and dermatoglyphics. Not one of these factors has enough significance to merit being weighed alone in making an overall personality and health assessment. Each represents some amount of influence or some aspect that needs to be considered.

Therefore, in order to make the most accurate evaluation of all, review each of those assessments. The chart that you filled out in the third chapter is a good place to start.

Remember, your hands reveal the positive qualities you possess, as well as the areas in which you need improvement. By interpreting the messages found in your hands, you can feel reassured knowing that your occupation, lifestyle, or health is supported by the lines, shape or coloring you have in your hands. Feeling that reassurance is like getting a pat on the back—with your own two hands!

The following list was compiled to simplify the process of making an overall assessment, particularly of vocational preferences. It is a list of more than fifty occupations and vocations. Check to see if the symbols found in your hands denote an occupation compatible with the one in which you are now. If you find that your own career does not match the one that your hands denote would be suitable, it may be that the two professions have some similarities that make them personally satisfying. Or, perhaps this may give you a clue as to why you've been feeling like a misfit at your present job. It is not necessary to assume the exact profession suggested in your hands, but perhaps you should consider one that is more compatible.

All of the professions listed below belong to one of two categories—the specialist or the generalist. Generally, the specialist is someone who works with parts—specializing in a particular field, task or service. The generalist, however, is quite able to use "holistic" thinking to perceive the whole. An example of a generalist is the head of a company, who is responsible for overall operations. This individual is likely to use specialists to get the work done.

Vocational Assessments

Actor/Actress Fingers should be longer than the hand proper and conical tips are preferred. You need a strong, high Mount of Apollo, as well as Mount of Mercury, and your Mercury finger should be long and well developed.

Adventurer Spatulate, smooth fingers with a long thumb tip are desirable. The lines of life and head should be widely separated at the start. The Upper Mount of Mars and Mount of Jupiter are usually prominent with a bulging and wide Plain of Mars. There are strong head and heart lines without a line of liver, and if there is a liver line present, it is a very clear, straight one.

Analyst Large hands with long knotty fingers are usually present, as is a strong second thumb phalange with a decided knot. Second phalanges of all fingers will be longer than normal.

Animal Worker (Veterinarian, farmer, etc.) Strong Mounts of Venus and Apollo are preferred, as well as a long, strong heart line. First finger phalanges are better when they are shorter than normal.

Architect Square-tipped fingers, often spatulate, are a positive sign. Usually, there are long square nails and a long second thumb phalange. The Mounts of Venus and Apollo (for art), and the Mount of Mercury (for calculation) should be accompanied by a strong head line.

Art For those artists interested in making a decent living from their craft, square-tipped fingers with a line of Apollo ending on Mercury is a very positive sign. Often there is a straight head line and the Mount of Mercury is at least equal to the Mount of Apollo.

Art and Science Fingertips nearly square and a second finger knot is common. The Mount of Apollo is thrown toward the Mount of Mercury. A triangle on the Mount of Apollo helps. The line of Apollo should end between the third and fourth fingers, or even on Mercury. A very positive formation is a line of Apollo with a triple fork at the end.

Artist A fate line should end on the Mount of Apollo with a branch from the head line to the same mount. It is best when the Apollo line comes from the life line. You may fail in art if you have poorly developed Apollo and Venus mounts. A broken or confused line of Apollo increases your chance for failure. A possible lack of persistency is shown by a poor head line with a short thumb tip. Exaggerated Jupiter and Apollo mounts may indicate envy without talent! For painters, conical tips, especialy on the third finger, are needed. Sculptors should have square tips. For imaginative, original art work, a strong Mount of Luna with somewhat soft hands and a drooping head line indicate success.

Astronomer Long, knotty fingers with square or spatulate tips are preferred. Hard bony palms are also favorable. The Mounts of Saturn (seriousness) and Mercury are prominent. The head line is clear and long and the second phalanges of the thumb and fingers are extra long.

Business Often, there are elastic palms with square-tipped fingers that are longer than the palm. A long thumb tip increases willpower and a strong head line is needed. The Mount of Mercury should be highest of all and the fourth finger should be extra long. A line from the rascette to the Mount of Mercury will help insure success, as will a line from the head line. You need a strong liver line (or none at all) and fair fate and Apollo lines to be really successful. Large hands are also helpful.

Carpenter Wide palms and square hands make you a good worker. Square-tipped fingers will increase your creativity.

Chemist or Physicist The second finger and Mount of Saturn are finely shaped and prominent, although not exaggerated. Long, knotty fingers and somewhat thin hands are helpful. A scientist is likely to have narrow palms with an average to small hand size.

Clairvoyant Usually, this is a soft hand with short, smooth fingers. You don't need a large thumb. Mounts of Saturn, Mercury and Luna are quite large. Many minor lines cross other lines. A drooping, fragmented head line, along with a poor heart line (indicating poor circulation) are frequently found. A clear line of intuition, sometimes with an island on it at the start, or a line of liver beginning with an island, are also often found.

Composer of Music (See also Musician.) A composer should have a strong Mount of Mercury (for calculation) and square fingers rather than the conical or pointed fingers of the musician. Here, there is less of the Mount of Venus and more of the Mount of Luna.

Dental Assistant Generally, this person is found with narrow palms and slightly short fingers.

Dramatic Profession (See also Actor.) Square fingers without knots, or knots only on the second phalange, are preferred. A strong thumb tip is helpful for perseverance. High Jupiter, Apollo and Mercury mounts, and some Venus and Luna mounts may be present. The lines of the head and life line should be separate with a fork at the end of the head line.

Engineering You should have a large, wide, square palm with long knotty spatulate fingers and square nails. It helps if the second finger and a Mount of Saturn are predominant. Scientific markings on the Mount of Mercury help, as do a large Mount of Mars and a fine, straight head line.

Entrepreneur For those who wish to be self-employed, a first finger leaning toward the thumb and leaving a wide space between the index and second finger is desirable. Spatulate tips, knotted joint and short nails with a long thumb tip are good signs. The Mount of Jupiter is prominent and separation between the head and life line is a must. A long head line is desirable as are marks on the Mounts of Mars and the Plain of Mars.

Fame If that's your aim, you will benefit from a star on the Mount of Jupiter and another on the line of Apollo. Also positive is a clear line of fate from rascette to the Mount of Saturn, or still better, ending on Jupiter or Apollo. Two straight sister lines to the Mount of Apollo, touching the line of Apollo, are helpful. Lines of the head and heart should be long. All mounts but Saturn and Luna are pronounced. For intellectual or artistic success and fame, you would benefit from a high Mount of Luna, also.

Fanatic If you want to devote your life to a cause, you should have long, thin, smooth fingers, especially the index finger. There should be a line or branch from the head line curving up toward Jupiter, then turning and ending on the Mount of Saturn. If the second finger has an exaggerated first phalange, you may be capable of persecuting others on behalf of your cause.

Farmer Spatulate fingertips are preferred. Long thick nails are good for hardiness. A regular thumb, with a high Mount of Saturn will be helpful. There should be no lines of nervousness and few minor lines. For hunters, a strong Mount of Mars is desirable.

Inventor This person should have an elastic palm with long, knotted fingers and short nails. The fourth finger should be even longer. A long thumb will insure tenacity and Apollo and Mercury mounts should be prominent. It is desirable if the Mercury mount has downward lines from it. A slightly drooping head line with a triple fork is a reinforcing sign. There may be a lack of success if a second knot is absent, if the head line droops too much or if the Lunar mount is extra high.

Investigator This person needs curiosity and it is indicated by straggling fingers that are very flexible, showing light between. Short nails are helpful, as are Apollo, Mercury, and Lunar mounts, which are prominent. The lines of the head and heart are usually separated at the beginning.

Lawyer Lawyers will benefit from short nails with a dominant fourth finger. A long second phalange on the thumb (which denotes logic) is advantageous. Large Mercury and Mars mounts are helpful, too. There should be a forked head line that is separate from the life line at the beginning.

Magician For stage magic, long thin fingers that may be crooked are a positive sign. The Mount of Mercury is prominent. A lower Mount of Luna will help the imagination.

Mathematician Usually, there are dry, hard palms with long, knotted fingers and an extra-long fourth finger. The Mercury mount is predominant and sometimes the Saturn is also. The second phalanges of the fingers are extra long. A very straight head line is positive if there is little development of the Luna and Apollo mounts.

Mechanical Arts The hand proper is longer than the fingers, which have square tips. Usually, the Mount of Mercury leans toward the Apollo line and a straight head line is present.

Medical The sign of the medical stigmata—four to seven downward lines on the Mount of Mercury—is positive for nurses, doctors, physicians or surgeons. A large-handed doctor is a physician with a fine bedside manner. A small-handed doctor wants to heal humankind.

Mercenary To be a revolutionary or a fighter, you need a square palm with short smooth fingers that are spatulate. Broad short nails and plenty of hair on the backs are helpful. Upper Mount of Mars must be prominent. Sometimes very red lines are seen.

Military The hand proper is longer than the fingers that have square tips. The Mount of Mars has no markings, but should be prominent. A strong Mount of Venus or Jupiter is helpful. It is desirable that the three main lines are clear and distinct and that there are few minor lines. One deep line on the third phalange of the second finger denotes success.

Ministry A pointed first finger and short nails are preferred. A moderate Mount of Venus with strong head and heart lines are also helpful. A cross in the Quadrangle under the Mount of Saturn denotes success. Large hands indicate that the person will make a helpful friend to the entire congregation. Small hands show a desire to save the world.

Musician Moderately soft hands with long, smooth, conical fingers are desirable. The Mounts of Apollo, Luna and Venus should be well developed and the head line should droop slightly. There are generally slight knots and a strong Mount of Mercury.

Mystic It is advantageous for an occultist to have a well-formed cross in the Quadrangle under the Mount of Saturn for it is the symbol of exceptional occult powers. This is called the Mystic Cross.

Navy Long, knotty fingers are evident, especially the third, which must be longer than average. A large Mount of Luna is present and is usually lined. For advancement, a large thumb tip should be seen, along with life and head lines, which are separated at the beginning. The head line that is drooping at the end is also a plus. Ship commanders will benefit from hard hands.

Nun or Monk Often a pointed index finger with a good Mount of Jupiter in a smooth, narrow, thin hand with long, smooth, pointed fingers is found. Always, the skin is very smooth. All mounts are insignificant, except the Mount of Jupiter.

Nurse Nurses need elastic palms with long knotty fingers that are either spatulate or square. There are usually abnormally broad nails that indicate great tolerance and a strong stomach. A strong Mount of Mercury with the sign of medical stigmata is positive, as are strong Mounts of Venus and Jupiter. Healthy head and heart lines and no worry lines are desirable.

Occult Sciences Thin palms with long smooth fingers, especially the first phalange, are preferred. The Mounts of Luna, Mercury and Saturn are prominent. A drooping head line and a definite line of intuition can also be helpful. The Mystic Cross and a triangle on the Mount of Luna, if it is well formed, denote success.

Outdoor Life and Sports Naturalists and athletes will benefit from good-sized fingers and large, hardy hands with spatulate tips. Many times there is a long third finger. The lines of the head and heart should be separate and there should be no worry lines. The mounts are low, except for Mars, and there are only the three major lines present.

Orator For politicians, diplomats, etc., the lines of the head and life separate at the start. The Mounts of Jupiter (statesman), Apollo (golden-mouthed), or Mercury (clear, practical politician) will be helpful. These mounts can be located in either hand. The line of the heart and the Mount of Venus should be in good shape for sincerity. If the line of the head is long, forked and slightly drooping, it is a helpful sign. This slope and a Mount of Luna infuses speech with more poetry than common sense.

Philosopher These are thin hands with hard palms and very long and knotted fingers. Often the first and fourth finger are conical and the others are spatulate.

Physician See Medical.

Poet (See also Writer.) Pointed fingers are best, although conical fingers are also positive. Poets are apt to have a long thin thumb tip and thin soft palms. The Apollo, Luna and Venus mounts are prominent. Usually, the heart line is drooping and it is often chained or has islands, which indicate a desire to express through poetry.

Politician (See also Orator.) Local politics usually requires an exaggerated Mount of Mercury. If the head line droops and the Upper Mars Mount is much lined, it may indicate a capacity to be quite aggressive with opponents.

Salesperson These people will be more successful if their hands are small and their fingers are slightly long. Salespeople are apt to have hard hands.

Seer or Saint A transparent hand with almond-shaped nails is preferable. Often the fingers are very pointed and smooth. A high mount and a line of intuition are helpful. The Mystic Cross should be present in both hands.

Speculator Here, we find slightly conical fingertips, especially in the fourth finger. No knots are found and the third finger is longer than normal. The Mounts and Plain of Mars are highly developed. Usually, there is a long head line, which droops slightly.

Surgeon (See also Medical.) The surgeon needs a palm with long, spatulate, knotted fingers. He or she will also benefit from excellent Mounts and Plain of Mars.

Teacher Teachers should have square-tipped, knotted fingers, and a long, well-shaped thumb. The Mounts of Mars and Mercury are predominant. The lines of the head and heart are extremely fine and the head line is slightly separate from the life line at the start. A positive Mount of Apollo shows higher intellect.

Traveler Travelers require thick elastic hands with square palms and short, smooth, spatulate fingers. A pronounced third finger is helpful when travel poses danger. There should also be prominent travel lines at the base of the life line.

Writer Important for an aptitude in literature are long first and fourth fingers, especially if they are conical. It is preferable if the Mercury and Apollo mounts are prominent. For poetry and fiction, the Mounts of Venus and Luna should be pronounced. A somewhat forked head line that is drooping slightly may also be evident. A small downward line on the first joint of the first finger can be positive, as can a line from the rascette to the Mount of Apollo, which assures success.

As noted before, none of these characteristics mean you have to be in one of these professions. However, they may indicate a predisposition or ability in that field.

The wonder of hand analysis is that it can tell us so much about ourselves that we wouldn't otherwise know. We all have an area of health or personality that needs improvement, or an area of our lives that we would like to concentrate on. Hand analysis can indicate those areas to us. This book is my gift to you so that you can gain that knowledge—through your hands.

Bibliography

Anderson, Mary. *Palmistry, Your Destiny in Your Hands*, Weiser (New York), 1973.

Bright, J.S. *Palmistry Made Easy*, Jaico Publishing (Bombay, India).

——. *A Dictionary of Palmistry*, Jaico Publishing (Bombay, India).

Broekman, Marcel. *The Complete Encyclopedia of Practical Palmistry*, Prentice-Hall (New Jersey), 1972.

Cheiro. *Complete Palmistry*, Dell Publishing (New York), 1968.

Frith, Henry. *Palmistry Secrets Revealed*, Wishire Book Company Hollywood, California), 1969.

Gettings, Fred. *Palmistry Made Easy*, Wilshire Book Company (Hollywood, California), 1968.

——. *The Hand and the Horoscope*, Triune Books (London, England).

Hipskind, Judith. *Palmistry, The Whole View*, Llewellyn Publications (St. Paul, Minnesota), 1977.

Hoffman, Elizabeth. *Palm Readings Made Easy*, Simon & Schuster (New York), 1971.

Jaegers, Bevy. *You and Your Hand*, Aries Productions (St. Louis).

——. *Stars in Your Hands*, Aries Productions (St. Louis), 1974.

Jennings, Alice Denton. *Your Hand Tells All*, E.P. Dutton (New York), 1942.

Lehman, Leona. *The Key to Palmistry*, Bell Publishing (New York), 1963.

MacKenzie, Nancy. *Palmistry for Women*, Warner Books, Inc. (New York), 1973.

Niles, Edith. *Palmistry*, Tower Publications (New York).

——. *Palmistry, Your Fate in Your Hands*, HC Publishers (New York), 1969.

——. *Complete Hand Reading for the Millions*, Sherborne Press (Los Angeles), 1970.

Ojha, Pandit Ashutosh. *Palmistry for All*, Hind Pocket Books (Delhi, India), 1972.

Peckman, Elizabeth. *Your Future in Your Hands*, Ace Publishing Company (New York), 1968.

Saint-Germain, Count de. *The Practice of Palmistry for Professional Purposes*, Newcastle Publishing (North Hollywood, California), 1973.

Sheridan, Jo. *What Your Hands Reveal*, Award Books (New York), 1969.

Sorell, Walter. *The Story of the Human Hand*, Bobbs-Merrill Company, Inc. (New York), 1967.

Squire, Elizabeth. *Palmistry Made Practical*, Wilshire Book Company. (North Hollywood, California), 1969.

Steinbach, Martin. *Medical Palmistry*, University Books (Seacaucus, New Jersey), 1975.

Wilson, Joyce. *The Complete Book of Palmistry*, Bantam Books (New York), 1971.

DEVELOP YOUR PSYCHIC SKILLS

Enid Hoffman

Psychic skills are as natural to human beings as walking and talking and are much more easily learned. Here are the simple directions *and* the inside secrets from noted teacher and author Enid Hoffman.

Develop Your Psychic Skills gives you a broad overview of the whole field of psychic experiences. The exercises and practices given in this book are enjoyable and easy to do. Use them to strengthen and focus your own natural abilities and turn them into precise, coordinated skills. You'll be amazed at the changes that begin to happen in your life as you activate the right hemisphere of your brain, the intuitive, creative, psychic half, which has been ignored for so long.

This book shows you how your natural psychic powers can transform your life when you awaken the other half of your brain. It teaches you techniques for knowing what others are doing, feeling and thinking. You can see what the future holds and explore past lives. You can learn to locate lost objects and people. You can become a psychic healer. It is all open to you.

Develop occasional hunches into definite foreknowledge. Sharpen wandering fantasies and daydreams into clear and accurate pictures of events in other times and places. Choose what you want to do with your life by developing your psychic skills. When you finish this book you'll realize, as thousands of others have using Enid Hoffman's techniques, that the day you began to develop your psychic skills was the day you began to become fully conscious, fully creative and fully alive.

ISBN 0-914918-29-X
183 pages, 6½" x 9¼", paper, $9.95

EXPAND YOUR PSYCHIC SKILLS

Enid Hoffman

In this sequel to her best-selling *Develop Your Psychic Skills*, Hoffman shows you how to use your inate psychic abilities to improve your daily life and your relationships with other beings. Huna concepts, along with dozens of techniques, exercises, games and meditations are included to help you fully utilize your inner resources. Psychic healing, working with crystals and gemstones, communicating telepathically with people and animals, heightening creative powers, and eliminating old behaviors that are interfering with your personal growth are just a few of the areas covered.

ISBN: 0-914918-72-9
144 pages, 6½" X 9¼", paper

$9.95